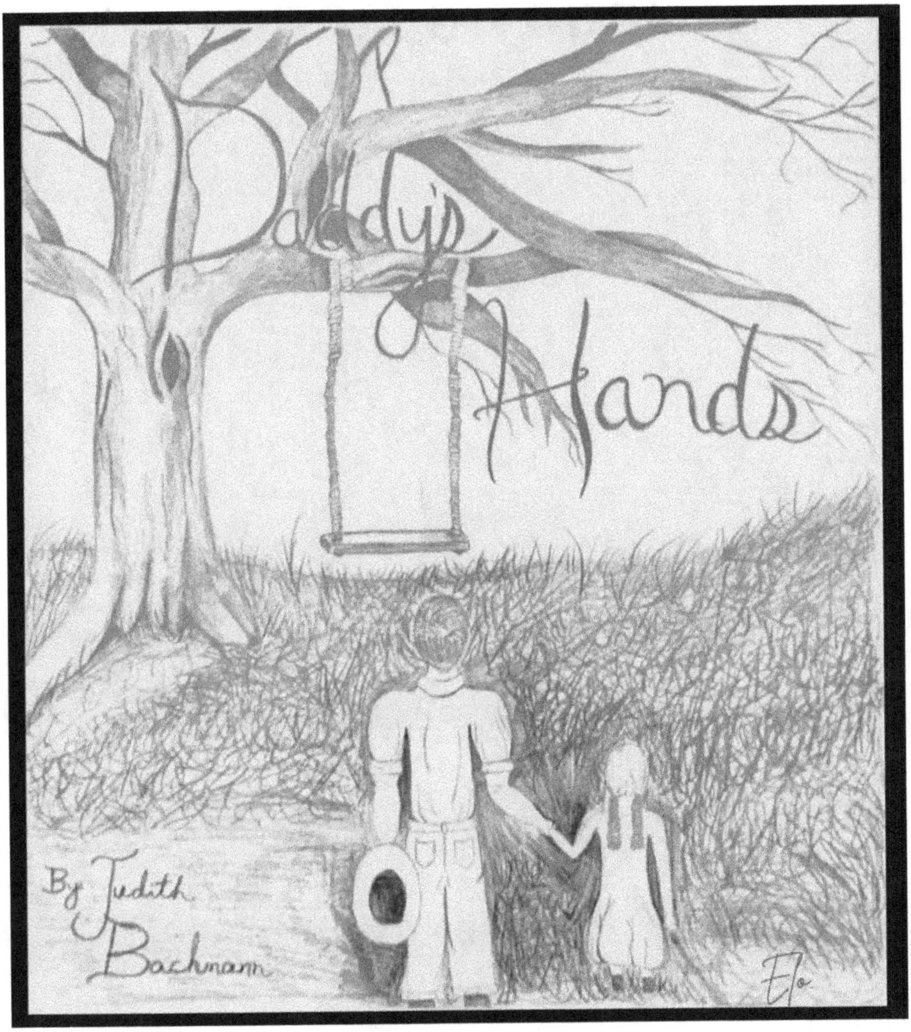
Daddy's Hands
By Judith Bachmann
Elo

Daddy's Hands

By

Judith Bachmann

Paperback ISBN: 978-1-965501-23-8

Hardcover ISBN: 978-1-965501-22-1

Published by Silicon Book Publishers

www.siliconbookpublishers.com

Table of Contents

"A TIME FOR EVERYTHING"

Ecclesiastes 3,
New International Version

There is a time for everything,
and a season for every activity under the heavens:
² a time to be born and a time to die,
a time to plant and a time to uproot,
³ a time to kill and a time to heal,
a time to tear down and a time to build,
⁴ a time to weep and a time to laugh,
a time to mourn and a time to dance,
⁵ a time to scatter stones and a time to gather them,
a time to embrace and a time to refrain from embracing,
⁶ a time to search and a time to give up,
a time to keep and a time to throw away,
⁷ a time to tear and a time to mend,
a time to be silent and a time to speak,
⁸ a time to love and a time to hate,
a time for war and a time for peace.

⁹What do workers gain from their toil? ¹⁰I have seen the burden God has laid on the human race. ¹¹He has made everything beautiful in its time. He has also set eternity in the human heart, yet [a] no one can fathom what God has done from beginning to end. ¹²I know that there is nothing better for people than to be happy and to do good while they live. ¹³That each of them may eat and drink and find satisfaction in all their toil—this is the gift of God. ¹⁴I know that everything God does will endure forever; nothing can be added to it and nothing taken from it. God does it so that people will fear him."

The events we live through have a strong bearing on our lives, how we cope and the heritage we pass on. Dad was born in 1911 and a time to weep and a time to laugh, was often a vital part of his life. Those times strongly affected all of us who loved him. I see him in myself, my brother and my children. Thanks to the support of my brother Neil and my husband Fred through my times to weep the good memories and times to laugh live on.

Thank you! Fred and Neil.

"A TIME TO BE BORN AND A TIME TO DIE"

Part one

DeImptigen Switzerland August 2011

December 14th, 1911, what a miraculous time to be born. Stuart W. Swingruber, (Stu), my dad was born into a rapidly unfolding century, country and world. Stu, the youngest of 8 children was born to the 43year old wife of a naturalized Swiss immigrant.

William Howard Taft was the United States' President, and the future President Reagan was born, the US population had not yet reached one hundred million, federal spending was approximately 70 billion, and postage stamps were 2 cents. 1911 saw the invention of erector sets; Marie Curie made the discovery of elements of radium and Polonium, and women's right to vote was still almost 10 years away. Stu's Mother, my grandmother, would not have the right to vote for another 10 years. The atomic bomb was still 34 years ahead, and McDonald's 15-cent hamburger was a dream that belonged to 50 years in the future.

1877, in DeImptigen, Switzerland, Stu's grandfather Jakob Schwengruber died when Stu's father (Fred) was 12 or 13. His mother, a 45-year-old widow with 4 children, remarried soon after.

At 17, Stu's father, Fred Schwengruber (Swingruber) left DeImptigen, Switzerland alone. He had American sponsors, a local farming family, and they had employment waiting. Dad once told me how his father's job working on their farm allowed him to earn enough money to bring his family to this country.

Census records indicate that in 1883 or 1884 Fred sponsored his brother (Louis) and sisters Alice and Susan along with his step-father and mother (Susanna, Warren, Schwengruber Grossen) to join him in America. Fred's uncle Louis Schwengruber remained in Switzerland.

Dad used to laugh when remembering his dad telling him about the abundance of food in America when Fred first arrived. Fred (his dad) had become very ill. Not ill because it wasn't good, but because it was so rich and bountiful. The first breakfast had been so large that Fred was sure he would not eat again that day or perhaps, for several days, hence he ate accordingly. His diet in Switzerland for his first 17 years consisted mainly of bread, cheese, and goat's milk. He really needed to learn to adjust to ***"American bounty."***

Fred married Francis Marion Wood, the daughter of John and Mary Hague Wood, in January 1885.

Fred and Francis Marion Wood Swingruber 50 years later 1935

Fred and Francis had 8 children, 3 boys, then 4 girls, and then 10 years later, the youngest, Stu, my dad. One of Stu's older sisters,

Helen, born in 1895, had passed away from Rheumatic Fever as a young girl of 14 in 1909, two years before Stu's birth.

Mom often told me that Stu had always been very special to his mom. Thinking back it had been ten years since her last child was born and two years after the loss of Helen. Stu must have been a blessing to this woman in her mid-forties. Mom told me once that when Dad's mother was ill, and it was believed she was dying, Gramma struggled not to let go until Stu arrived to say goodbye. Dad would have been a young man of 28 or 29. Mom said that it was a very difficult time for Dad. It took him a while to ***"suck it up"*** and go say goodbye and be at her bedside. Gramma had been a Baptist and a member of the Baptist church in New Hartford, NY. Even though she died before I was born, I am very aware of her very deep faith and her influence on both Jessie (who remained a Baptist) and Dad.

As I follow today's news, I remember Dad telling me that his mother would speak about something that she found in reading her bible. She would tell him that when the bear steps on the turkey, it will mean the end of the world. She believed that it was somewhere referenced in her bible. How would one have known, when the bible was written, that centuries later, there would be a country called Turkey? Or that Turkey would have a relationship with today's Russia known as the bear?

Long after Dad's passing, my husband surprised me with a trip to Switzerland for our fiftieth wedding anniversary. On that visit in 2011, our guide told us that up until a few years before, it was a law that all people attend church on Sunday.

Mornings on our trip, as I gazed across the beautiful mountains, I could not help but notice, there across the valley, standing proudly nestled between the Rocky Craigs was a small white chapel. A chapel, accessible only to the climbers for fulfillment of that requirement. I found my thoughts wandering to the grandpa I never knew. I wondered if Grampa Fred, as a young boy in Switzerland while tending goats and sheep on the summer meadows, worshiped in a hillside chapel like that on Sundays.

DeImptigen Valley 2011

DeImptigen Valley, 2011

Dad was not a big Sunday morning churchgoer, but in the Methodist church (Mom's religion) in town, there are a lot of places touched by Dad's hands. The most prominent of those are the beautiful cathedral-style lights hanging from the ceiling in the sanctuary. Dad hung those, and I am not sure if he was ever paid or if it was a family donation. As I sit in worship, those lights are a constant reminder of my dad. He told me that during the thirties, when times were still hard from the 1929 crash, people would often pay the minister with chickens or a piece of beef.

Cathedral lights installed by Stu

After talking with Neil about my book he relayed to me the following believable story. It would seem that Neil was helping Dad when he was hanging those lights. Neil's job was to steady the tall step ladder as Dad was working 25 to 30 feet in the air, installing the lights from the ceiling. As usual, when helping Dad, it would seem to take forever, and it was easy for a young fella of 14 or 15 to become distracted. Apparently, that is what happened, and the ladder started to wobble. Dad was known to use some rather colorful language from time to time, and he let out a holler to Neil to pay attention and hang on to the ladder (Neil reported that Dad used the opportunity to expound with some of that language). In the meantime, what had distracted Neil's attention was that two or three "elders" of the church had arrived unannounced into the sanctuary within earshot of Dad's reprimand. Dad was not amused, but Neil always chuckled at getting one over on Dad. Sometimes, during church, a quiet smile crosses my face as I remember the story and think of those "elders" that I once knew.

Jessie, Stu's next oldest sibling, was just 9 or 10 when he was born. She told me once that she was furious when Stu was born, and she wouldn't even look at the new baby. She was angry because she had been kept at school until he arrived. The teacher had received a handwritten note from home. The note revealed that Jessie's mother was in labor, so Jessie and her sister Gladys, two-years older, should not come home yet. Imagine a home birth, with no text, no phone, no internet, most likely no running water, and simply a hand-carried note to the teacher of Jessie and Gladys. Just think, during that baby's lifetime, horse-drawn wagons and plows would be replaced by gas-powered cars and tractors, text and phones, and internet-replaced hand-carried notes. 1911 saw the first Indianapolis 500, and the first self-starting ignition was installed to eliminate the need for the hand crank. The Model T would evolve into high-performance engines and cars. There would be TV, video, DVR, and color motion pictures with sound. The Wright Brothers' airplanes would become super-sonic jets, stealth bombers, and drones, and a man would walk on the moon. Kate Smith would sing God Bless America, and patriotism would flourish. What a world and what wonders laid ahead for a blond, blue-eyed boy born to a Swiss immigrant and his wife. What an exciting world would unfold in his next 89 years.

Growing up, Stu learned to love and care for animals of all kinds. He spoke often of his "three-quarter" horse Nancy and how, with just his whistle, she would come running at a gallop. Without stopping, she allowed him to grab her mane and swing onto her back. No saddle, no reins, just a young boy on her back, hands in her mane, wind in his hair, galloping off to do whatever and wherever a young boy desired.

He also had a collie named Pal.

Dad was adamant that he would never put a collar on any of his dogs. He had found Pal in the woods once stranded because a stick on a tree had gotten between his collar and his neck. He never said so, but I have often wondered if he did not find Pal in time to save him.

Dad had a special whistle or a call for most of the animals he would come into contact with. A series of high whistles for a horse, a throaty **common bos** for the cows, a **heauah** for the dogs, even a **here pig, pig, pig**. At the same time, he was learning to care for and love animals. He also had to learn that some animals were raised to be food for the table. No grocery stores to pick up a piece of beef or a side of ribs. All lives were treated with dignity and respect. Even as I was growing up, we were never allowed to waste the kill from a hunt or fishing trip. Learning to dress out the kill and prepare it for the table was an important part of my learning process and my respect for guns and for the food we eat. My mind often wanders when in a grocery store looking to buy packaged chicken. Thinking back to our backyard, watching as the chickens were beheaded, then let to bleed out. The next step was to clean the insides and pluck off the feathers making it ready for mom to cook for supper. When mom prepared a wild animal, such as a pheasant or rabbit, she would add baking soda to the boiling water, let it foam up, then, rinse it, and start the cooking again with clean water. She said it took the gamey taste away.

In the early 60's, my husband and I purchased our home with a few acres. A neighbor rented the pasture from us to keep his donkey. Dad could stand on our back porch and make the sound of a donkey, and that shaggy, grey donkey in the pasture would answer. She would plant her front feet apart, lower and stretch out her neck. Then with a loud bray, actually answer him! It was one of the most comical things you could imagine hearing my dad and that donkey "talk" with each other.

There was another time that the neighbor's donkey supplied us with great entertainment. My brother, looking at the docile appearing donkey in our pasture decided he would see if he could go for a ride. Cautiously, he approached her and gently hopped on her back. Without a sound the donkey kicked her hind legs up sending my brother into the air, then unconcerned she walked out from under Neil leaving him to land seated on his butt on the ground.

Our new home had a large Box Alder tree with a rope swing hanging from it for the kids. It was in the backyard between our house and the pasture. Dad would get a running start down the porch steps, across the lawn, grab that rope with his hands, and swing himself upside down, wrapping his feet above him around the rope. Hanging there, he would laugh while the change from his pockets rattled to the ground. In his later years, as his Parkinson's claimed the use of his legs, it became harder and harder to remember Dad in that kind of physical shape. Thankfully, time has helped those long-ago memories to come, creeping back into my awareness, crowding out the trials of Dad's last few years.

As Dad grew older, he would sometimes need to be a resident of a nursing home. On good days, during my daily visits, we were able to spend time outside in the large yard that stretched across the back of the facility. There were huge old Maple trees that formed a canopy overhead of rich green leaves. That canopy was always filled with happy, chattering squirrels. There were the usual greys and also a few black ones. Sitting there one day with Dad in his wheelchair, the sun was softly filtering through the leaves. Dad had me gather a couple of small smooth stones. They had to be just big enough to fit into the palm of my hand. He then taught me to clap them together in such a way that sounded just like the chatter of the squirrels. Those stones clicking together would cause the squirrels to take notice and come to find out who was talking to them. We kept those stones hidden under the bushes so we could find them whenever we were able to spend time in the yard calling the squirrels and feeding them peanuts.

It was a beautiful sunny afternoon, and as I pulled into Dad's driveway. I noticed that his big grey garbage can was lying on its side. It had been tightly tucked into a corner between the steps and the porch. As I walked over to set it upright, I noticed that there was a sign taped to the front. ***"Do not disturb a possum is sleeping."*** Sure enough, to this day, I am not sure how the sign was posted or by whom, but there is no doubt that Dad had a hand in letting the possum take his nap.

As a young man, Dad worked for the local farmers. One day, on our usual trip to the doctor, we drove past a large housing development. He reminisced to me that in his youth, housing development was a ***"swamp."*** A swamp so massive that it had places where a cow could sink deep enough to render it unable to free itself. When one of the local farmers would have a cow come up missing, Dad would be contacted. The farmer would hire dad to lead his cow to safety. Dad was able to enter the swamp through paths he knew to be safe from his hunting and trapping experiences. Those experiences enabled Dad to return the cow to the safety of its pasture. He could never figure out how that "swamp' was drained dry enough to build on. He often wondered if they had water problems in their basements.

One of the sadder times for Stu was when his father, somewhere around 62 years of age, was stricken with an attack of appendicitis. Grampa Fred's Surgery in the 1920s necessitated Stu to quit school in the fall of his freshman year. The practice of Medicine is yet another area that evolved during Stu's lifetime. Certainly, today's surgery would hardly create such a hardship to a man in his

60s the way it did in the 1920s. Stu himself was 86 in 1996 when he had surgery for an aortic aneurysm, recovered, and was home in 6 days. Today there would be a rapid recovery, and all kinds of help would be available to keep that teenager in school. Most likely, today's 16-year-old would not have to quit school.

Dad never talked about why he quit school. It was mom who filled me in on the facts surrounding his father's surgery. In later years, however, the lady who had been his teacher at the time told me that she had gone to see Stu's dad in hopes that Stu would not have to quit school. She thought him to be quite bright and had a great future ahead of him. Dad had loved school and absorbed everything presented, even to the day he died. Needless to say, her efforts were in vain, and that little blond, blue-eyed boy's life had different things in store for him. He must *"suck it up"* and work the farm to sustain the family.

Dad's older brother Charles passed away due to Rheumatic Fever at the young age of 30. He had been sickly, and he and his family lived at the homestead. When Charles passed, Dad's widowed sister-in-law and two nieces remained living there. For Stu at 16, they became an additional part of his responsibilities. Dad was always sensitive to not "finishing" school. He would visibly "bristle" at even a hint of someone making fun of him. His three children were able to finish high school. Neil finished college and became a great teacher. All of his grandchildren also completed college. To the day he died, he absorbed everything he could; he loved to read. One of his happier times with the medical community was the removal of his cataracts. He could read again! The Reader's Digest, National Geographic, and the Jack London stories were among his favorites. Mom and Dad's books included a couple of birds and wildlife that they loved. Those books are on my shelf and referred to with fond memories quite often. The colorful photos and text about Cardinals and Orioles are among the many birds they fed in the backyard. They watched every spring for the Orioles to come back and build their nest until the old Elm was torn down. The graceful limbs of the Elm cascaded over our side lawn. One of those limbs proved perfect for the Orioles' nest in plain sight of mom's kitchen windows.

Part of the chores for Stu included cleaning the manure out of the Chicken coop. Mom told me that she and her best friend, Alma, went to see Alma's boyfriend, Stu. Picture two teenage girls trying to quietly sneak up on a young man 4 or 5 years older. Stu, with a shovel in hand, was cleaning the chicken droppings from their coop. I can almost hear the giggles that must have been stifled as those two tried to sneak up on Dad. Dad relayed that meeting to me. He recalled looking up to see ***the most beautiful pair of dark eyes he had ever seen.*** Those were the eyes of my mother. Mom's best friend lost her boyfriend to those eyes that very day, and for the next 65 years until Mom's death, they were together. Dad's eyes were a beautiful, brilliant crystal blue as were his sister Jessies'. I don't remember Gladys or Marian's eyes, but Dads were that beautiful crystal clear blue that, even in his late 80's, caught the attention of the nurses.

I inherited mom's dark eyes; Neil received the blue and many of dads' grandchildren inherited blue eyes. Blue and green eyes are also prevalent in the great-grandchildren, but Kooper, one great-grandchild in particular, has eyes so like dad's that it causes me to stop and pause.

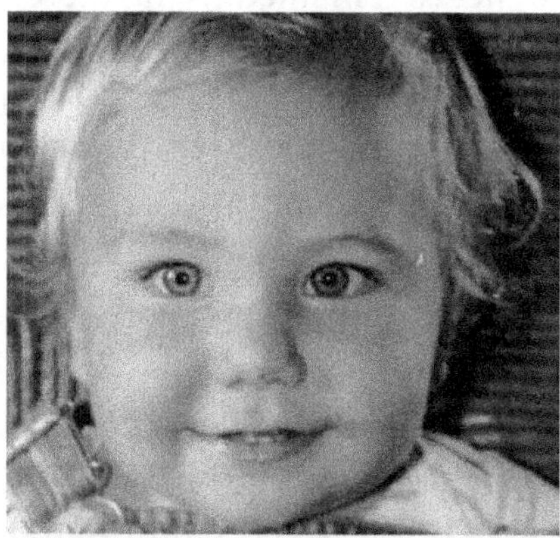

Jakson Kooper great grandson of Stu

<u>"A TIME TO PLANT AND A TIME TO UPROOT"</u>

Growing up on a small family farm, Dad learned to grow almost anything. At a time of no electric refrigeration and certainly no freezers or store-bought packaged items, potatoes, cabbages, squash, and beets needed to be grown and wintered in crocks buried in the ground. I have several crocks of varying sizes. To me, they are more than decorative. They are a reminder of my parents and the times of their youth. To Dad, growing up, they were a necessity of life. Animals for meat had to be slaughtered and preserved by smoking or with salt.

Jessie told me once that as a new bride in the early 1920s, it was her task to preserve the meat from a freshly killed cow with salt. She became sidetracked, and as a result, due to her negligence, all of the meat spoiled. Times were tough, and lessons were sometimes learned the hard way. It was obvious that this favored aunt of mine, somewhere in her 70's, still felt the sting of her hard-earned lesson. Farms in the early 20th century often had spring houses to keep food stuff cold, separate tool sheds, animal barns, and chicken coops. Dad's hands had to learn to grow tomatoes for canning, grapes to be squeezed for homemade juice or jam, and cucumbers for pickling. My China cabinet holds a cherished green, cut glass dish that was Dad's mom's. He smiled as he saw I had it while remembering that she had kept her homemade pickles in it on her kitchen table.

He would often relay to me little things like peas should be planted before Good Friday, corn should be knee-high by the fourth of July and Snow is the poor man's fertilizer. Thick corn husks and tough apple skins indicate a mean winter. The colors on a woolie caterpillar or if we saw skunks in early spring meant something, but for the life of me, I don't remember what. Red sky at night sailors delight, and red sky in the morning sailors take warning. There was also a little rhyme about planting seeds: ***"One for the cut-worm, one for the crow, one to rot, and one to grow."*** I used to think that Dad made those things up. Since his passing, one Sunday morning, while the scriptures were read, they actually included that rhyme. Once more, his mother's influence? Spring always reminds me of Dad's insistence regarding those little critters (peepers) that come alive and become vocal in the spring. Once, then twice, they need to be forced back by the return of cold weather before spring can come to stay. How comforting to me are the sounds they make. I will often hear my husband or one of my kids ask me, ***"Did you hear the peepers"?*** They all know that I believe spring is not here to stay until I hear the peepers that third time.

Leonard and Rose Wood were neighbors for a while when we lived in the house on Main Street. Leonard was known by everybody as Woody, and Rose was a small-framed woman with black hair. They had two children: a son that I have no memory of and a daughter, Lois. Lois had survived a bout with Polio that left her left leg with a limp. Both Rose and Lois were very accepting of a little girl popping in on them to say hello. Rose always seemed to me to be a very "refined" lady. Woody was not a very large man in height but seemed to be very strong. He was the first person that I remember with a tattoo. I don't remember exactly what they were, but I do remember that they stood out on his very stout calf and along both arms. Dad had explained that Woody had been a merchant marine and many of those fellows had tattoos. He gently explained that ladies really didn't get them. (early training on what he expected from me) Mom told me once that Rose's family had been "well off" and hadn't really approved her marriage to a "merchant marine". Woody and Rose lived in what seemed to me to be a very large green house. In later years, it burned to the ground and only left memories from a small girl's perspective. As you entered from the front, there were two big doors that could disappear into the walls separating the two front rooms. At the back door, there was a large kitchen where I most often popped in to find Rose and Lois. Since I was too young to go to the neighbors along the road, I would cross the lot between houses and enter through the back door. I am not aware of when they moved or where they went. Fifty-plus years later, I was able to locate Lois in Alabama. I needed some information to clear the title to Dad's house for sale after his death. As she replied to my inquiry about the title, she remembered the little girl from next door with the beautiful long black ringlets.

A short distance across the meadow, the homestead of Woody and Rose included a large barn with lots of acreage for pasture. The history of the town tells me that that barn I loved had once been a brewery. Brocket's Brewery, I was told, brewed a pretty good brew. Dad operated that farm when I was small. Mom told me once that she made Dad give up farming because she thought a girl would not like it. I don't know for sure, but I wonder if perhaps Woody or Rose passed away and the family moved. Perhaps Dad had wanted to buy Woody's farm as that would explain Mom's story.

Woody's Barn as seen from our yard.

I can still close my eyes and see Woody's barn. The hay loft was on the ground floor with the stables on the lower level. You entered up the sloped walk and through the huge wooden front doors. Crossing the threshold, you were immediately aware of the sweet-smelling golden yellow bales of hay piled high. The bales, held together tightly with strong bailing twine, always held a warmth even on the coldest days. Those heavy, oblong bales were always stacked so high that you could barely see the streams of sunlight flowing through the one window way up in the peak of the roof.

In the front corner, just inside the large doors, was the wooden ladder that would take me from the ground-level hayloft down to the lower level. To get to the lower level, there was a small opening in the front right beside the door. A rough hand-hued ladder fastened next to the wall, down along the outside of one of the stalls housing Woody's big draft horses. Dad would go down ahead of me, and as I would start down, I always knew Dad's big hands would reach up and steady me around my waist to make sure I would safely reach the lower level. The wooden boxed stalls that housed Woody's huge plow horses were located on that lower level. The stanchions that held the heads of the cows were located front to back through the middle of the basement. That is where the cows stood to be milked and to receive their grain. The "herd" was most likely less than a dozen and certainly smaller in number than most today. It did, however, include Popeye, a big old cow that mom really did not like. Black and white Popeye had huge eyes that "bugged out," and Mom believed she was mean. The lower level emptied out directly into the barnyard, pasture with fields that meandered all the way to the woods beyond. Dad seemed to know every weed and plant. Once in a while he would take me with him, and we gathered some of those plants for the table. He and I would find the horseradish that grew in the pasture alongside the barn wall to grind it up for the table. Today, when I purchase a bottle of horseradish for my pot roast, memories of Dad and I together flood my mind. There was a spring that we went and picked what Dad called cow slips. They still grow in the wet areas around home. They are small green-leaved plants with yellow flowers sticking straight up in their center. They taste a lot like spinach or dandelions.

Dad often spoke of beautiful yellow roses that his mother grew in their yard.

Stu with mother at homestead on Woods Highway, Whitestown, NY

In later years, he had beautiful roses at his home in Westmoreland.

Dad's roses at home in Westmoreland

Dad kept in touch with his many farmer friends and would stop to see them often as they were in the barn milking cows. Cows need to be milked twice a day, every day, morning and night. He knew most of the men who earned their living as farmers. He would purchase the straw and manure he needed for those roses. Cow manure seemed to be a great asset for his roses, and the straw was to bed them down, covering them in cold weather. Dad would often take me with him on those visits, and I learned my way around the farming life. I will never forget those visits, walking down the rows of black and white cows, sometimes in front of them as their big eyes watched me pass. I was fascinated by the round metal water dishes attached to the outside of the stanchion. Inside those dishes was a slotted lever. As the cow would drink, her nose would press down on the lever, and the bowl would refill with water. Sometimes, depending on the layout of the barn, I would walk between the rows, between their backsides, always staying clear of their tails, swishing back and forth, keeping watch to avoid getting splashed as the cows relieved themselves into the gutters. The gutters were just cement indentations at the back of the cow where her manure landed. Those would need to be cleaned out by hand. Some of the more modern barns had a conveyer set into the gutter that would move the manure to the end for removal. There were always cats around at milking time. They would come close, sitting on their haunches, waiting for the farmer to squirt some fresh milk into their mouths or into their pans for them to enjoy. It amazes me that I now read that cats should not be given milk. At that time, milking by hand or using individual milking machines was the norm. For a farmer to milk by hand, he would sit very close to the cow and within reach of the cow's udder. Often resting his head on her side, he would then firmly squeeze and then, with a downward motion, strip each of her teats of milk one by one. The machines were used one cow at a time. The machines were silver in color and had enough suction cups for each teat. The farmer would attach and let the machine do the work. Each cow one by one. Often, I would pop in to say hello to the farmer's wife. There, in her kitchen, after milking, those machines were washed and turned upside down on her drain board to dry at the kitchen sink. Gleaming silver representations of the involvement of the farmer's wives. Often, the farmer would have a cooler where he kept his special cans full of milk until he had a load to transport to the plant for processing.

Years later, I had the opportunity to visit a milking parlor and

share my unique experience with Dad. 12 or 16 cows being milked at a time, standing in rows opposite each other. Ramps for them to walk up to be positioned back to back to each other. Long hoses with milking machine capacity were then attached to the cow's udders. The pure white milk flowing through plastic tubes into the shiny stainless cooler was never touched by human hands. The milk was kept cool there and stored until the tanker milk truck arrived. Gone were the days when the farmer had to transport milk cans by wagon or truck to the milk plant. Water for the cows flowed automatically, and the waste in the gutters no longer needed hand shoveling, but conveyor belts moved it along and out of the barn. Quite a change from those days of visiting Dad's farmer friends in the forties and fifties. I couldn't wait to share it with my dad, who, as usual, was eager to hear about the new way.

In later years when dad was pretty much limited in what he could do. I asked for his help, I mistakenly thought I was doing him a favor. Outside in my yard, he showed me how to trim my roses. It worked for a while, with Dad sitting in his wheelchair telling me which stems to cut and which to keep. Soon, however, in his gruff way of handling things, he said, ***"Take me home."*** Knowing better than to argue, we were soon on our way. All he said was, ***"I can't stand being so useless."*** He had been upset because he wasn't able to help me more than just instruct. He had hoped to get out of the wheelchair and cut them himself.

It was odd to me that there always seemed to be sweet peas growing in the backyard or on the table in mid-summer. It became clear, however, that on July 7, 1934, mom's wedding bouquet had been homegrown sweet peas. When Mom was in the nursing home on their anniversary, Dad had been unable to grow sweet peas. That day, I picked Dad up to visit Mom. He was all decked out, dressed in his brown suit and tie, complete with a vest, ready to celebrate their day with his bride of 63 years. However, we did need to make a stop. Along the way, beside the road, was a patch of wild Sweet Peas in the colors of beautiful pinks and lavender. Dad had been watching them bloom as we had traveled for previous visits, and he knew exactly where we could find them. A bouquet of Sweet Peas was picked and proudly taken to Mom at the nursing home.

July 7, 1934

July 7, 1984

They were like a couple of kids on that day, July 7, 1984. Anyone knowing my dad, would never think of him being a romantic. They had been married for 50 years, and we were celebrating that occasion at my home. We had over 50 people attending. Mom and Dad had arranged to have a favored minister perform a renewal of their wedding vows. Fred had constructed a wooden arch for the yard, and it was decorated in blue and yellow tissue flowers by our daughters. Under that arch decorated in yellow (for 50 years) and soft blue, Mom and Dad renewed their vows. Mom's brother and his wife were attendants, and our oldest daughter read the scripture.

Following a buffet meal, holding the knife together like a newly married couple. they cut their three-layer wedding cake. Decorated with yellow and blue frosting flowers.

That wedding cake had been the highlight of mom's day. She later told me that she had never had a wedding cake and that she was overjoyed with the one decorated with yellow and blue that stood on a table in my back yard.

Laughing mom even pushed a piece of the cake into dad's face. I don't think that I had ever seen them fool and laugh as they did that day or ever after.

Esther my mom, Stu's wife died in February of 1998. That summer Jennifer, our oldest daughter, and Mom and Dad's oldest granddaughter planted sweet peas at her grave. Those seeds did not sprout or show any signs of life -- until 2 ½ years later when Stu was placed in the grave beside her. The following spring and every year since the sweet peas have not only sprouted but have blossomed profusely every July 7th.

Gravestone of Esther Charlotte Dowsland Swingruber and Stuart W. Swingruber, Westmoreland Cemetery, Sweet Peas in blossom.

"A TIME TO KILL AND A TIME TO HEAL"

Dad loved to hunt and fish. Some of my fondest memories are of being with him on the trout stream in early spring. I would be awakened by the coffee perking on the stove, its' aroma filling the house. Either Dad or Mom would call me, and after a quick cup of coffee, Dad, Neil, and I would head off for the trout stream. Trout season always opened on April 1, and it was important to be on the creek at daylight. Through sleepy eyes, I would be surrounded by nature's early signs of spring. We usually went to the Oriskany Creek in Waterville for the first day. Parked on the edge of the road near the bridge, we would unload our gear and start over the bank down to the creek side. Most often, there would still be glistening white patches of snow tucked between the scrub willows, with the almost neon green skunk cabbage peeking up. The willows would begin to show their signs of spring, sprouting their fuzzy yellow caterpillar-like tips. I was always able to be decked out in my own hip boots and hat and had my own pole at a very young age.

If I was going to be part of those fishing trips, I needed to learn a few things. Dad taught me to thread the fish line through the eyes on the pole and add a hook and some sinkers. The hook and sinker are in place, and I need to add a worm. Once caught, I was to dress my own fish. Once dressed and split open, Mom would take over. She had a favorite iron skillet and would fry the trout nice and crisp for the family to enjoy a delicious meal.

Dad, with my brothers and I, picked those worms (nightcrawlers) by flashlight after dark from our lawn and sometimes the local golf course. A warm, gentle spring rain was just the right environment for picking worms. Dad always believed that the weather would break enough for us to be able to find those worms in time for the opening day of the Trout season. Dad had made a wooden box that we filled with leaves from the big maple trees on the front lawn. That box kept in a dark place with the bedding of moist leaves would be just the place to keep the worms we picked. They would be just the ticket to add to the hook in anticipation that a brown or a sassy brook trout would find it appealing. I can still see my dad, his long flyrod in hand, wading knee-deep into the stream, positioning the worm in the swirling water to just the right spot to catch the attention of those fish. He could not do that, though, unless his tongue was firmly placed between his lips.

I never knew us to purchase bait except for minnows when we were going lake fishing for Pike. Any worms we needed were stored in the leaves in their box behind our house. If we needed soft-shelled crabs, we stopped at the neighboring farms where there were still abandoned ice ponds. As usual, Dad had built his own tool for harvesting them. Leftover wood and pieces of the screen were put together to form a kind of "net." About two feet square at the front opening tapering down and rounded at the back. The old ice ponds were fairly shallow now and were full of soft-shelled crabs. Retrieving those crabs required wading into the water knee-deep, plunging the homemade screen into the water, and carefully moving it along the bottom toward the bank. When raised, there would be dozens of soft-shelled crabs and often some bass bugs or perch bugs. They would be carefully removed (the backs of the crabs were indeed soft) and placed into our pails for some fun time catching bass, perch, or pike.

Dad talked about those ponds when they had been the site of cutting ice blocks during the winter years. I am not sure how big the ice blocks were or how much they weighed. The Westmoreland 200-year book references those ice ponds and indicates that they produced 5,000 cakes of ice. In the days before homes had refrigerators, families used ice boxes to keep their foods cool. Mom had an electric refrigerator, but her mother never did. Gramma's "ice box" was about 3 or 4 feet high with three doors. It stood off the kitchen behind a door on a small landing at the top of the stairs leading to the cellar. As I remember it must have been made of oak with silver colored latches. The one door to the right side opened up and down the length of the box. An ice block would just fit into that side vertically. The other side had two doors to keep food cool. The ice blocks that Dad and the other men cut during the winter had been stored in buildings, packed in sawdust to reduce melting. Those ice blocks from the storage were delivered house to house, one at a time, filling home ice boxes for early forms of refrigeration. Dad explained that he would help cut those blocks and lift them out with large tongs. Just one of the many additional ways that my father earned money to feed his family. We were not very old when my grandmother, still without a refrigerator got an ice delivery for that ice box standing in the cellarway. Traffic was so different on the roads in the 40s. As kids, on hot summer days, we would follow the truck of the ice man. He would toss us chips, most likely to keep us from chipping our own and wrecking his ice for delivery.

Also, at harvest time great, stake rack trucks overflowing with fresh picked peas, still on their vines headed for canning at the canning factory on Rt. 233. Passing by, they were also fair game for us kids. Fresh, bright green pea pods, hanging from their vines, still warm from the sun, dangling over the sides of the truck. Those pods seemed to be waiting for us to pull them from the truck, split them open, and eat.

Dad also loved to hunt. The times when he grew up often included fresh game, a staple in the family's supper. We were taught at an early age that you do not kill unless you use the meat. I fondly remember the many hours walking with him in the fields of gold and yellow in the fall, flushing out beautifully colored pheasants. Or tracking rabbits through the fresh white snow of winter. I always had the beautiful tail or neck feathers of a pheasant and a "lucky" rabbit's foot. I was taught to recognize the tracks of rabbits or deer, cats or dogs, and many other animals. Each left markings of its own in the snow, telling me which way it was headed. When I show my grandchildren the tracks in our yard, they are hard-pressed to believe that Gramma would really know which are the neighbors' cat tracks and which are the rabbits'. Especially that Gramma would know which way the rabbit was running.

Thank you, dad!

There were a couple of times that the result of the hunt was not suitable to be used as part of our dinner menu. Dad, when dressing out a rabbit would always check the color of the liver and kidneys. If he found yellowish spots, he knew that the animal was not healthy and that the meat should not be eaten. The only other time I remember was one winter morning when our dogs flushed out a rabbit, and after it was shot, we noticed something very different. The rabbit had somehow gotten caught in the ring of a canning jar and, unable to free itself, had grown inside the ring. Dad felt that it was a blessing that the rabbit had been killed as the ring was beginning to grow into the rabbit's skin. Dad took it to the local paper, and all three of us appeared in the news, complete with a picture.

"A TIME TO TEAR DOWN AND A TIME TO BUILD"

Westmoreland, New York, in the late 1940s and early 1950's, was a great place for me to grow up. It seemed a relatively quiet place, even though there were several thriving businesses. Those businesses included a gas station, a couple of stores (one owned by Les Hull and one by Ms. Wiggins), a canning factory, an antique shop, a milk processing plant, a blacksmith shop, and a couple of other businesses. There was also a man who sold foodstuff from a van. He traveled house to house. Jay Burrows and his van stopped at our house, and Mom did business with him. Jay had a wooden leg and always seemed to be pleasant. His van looked like a giant brown hot dog. He had a handle beside his steering wheel that opened the folding doors on the passenger side, allowing you to step in and up to the "store" level. Once inside, you turned to the left, and behind the area where the driver sat were wooden shelves that held the foodstuff he had for sale. He even had meats for sale, which hung from the ceiling on hooks. I am not sure that the board of health today would allow his business to operate. There were two establishments that sold liquor and one church on Main Street where I attended Sunday school. During those years, It was determined that the New York State Thruway would have an exit at Westmoreland. Everyone was sure that because of that, the town would grow at a rapid pace. Not everyone was happy, though, as some of the farmers had the Thruway cut their acres into two parcels. For me, it meant that the big old house on a hill where we sometimes went sliding was going to be eliminated. That house had been occupied by Les Hull and his wife, who ran the store in town. Also, during that time, the Oneida County Airport was established just beyond the Town limits. That airport was the base for Robinson Airlines. Airplanes overhead were a novelty, and we would often run to the front lawn to watch them as they flew overhead. One afternoon, as I watched, I realized that the plane overhead did not look quite right. It wasn't very long after that we heard the news. That plane had crashed about 5 miles from my house. My older brother, a fireman at the time-responded to the crash. It left him with some disturbing memories.

The largest employer in town was the "Westmoreland Malleable Iron Company." That business had been established in Westmoreland in 1850, and generations of men worked there. Most of the Mom's brothers, her dad, and even my great-granddad worked in that foundry. My dad worked there for a while.

Much of my time was spent exploring the sights and sounds of "my town." To me, the main streets, East and West, seemed divided into sections. West of the intersection with Rt. 233 was known as up street. East from that intersection to the intersection with Furnace Street was known as Main Street. Main Street was lined with giant old Elm trees, their graceful arching branches seeming to hover over the street. It was funny that to the East on Main, there were Elms, but to the West, it was Maples that guarded the road edges with their green umbrellas of leaves. Even on the warmest of days, there was always shade for my walk. From the intersection of Furnace Street and Main St. to the cemetery, it was a mixture of those beautiful trees. Our lawn had a big Elm on the side lawn, two Maples on the road edge, and a streetlight on the east corner of the driveway. Many times, in later years, when I would need to arrive at Mom and Dad's in the middle of the night, I would be most grateful to see that streetlight's soft glow lighting the difficult way. One of those Maples had a large hollow on the roadside that was big enough for me to sit in, thinking and watching the traffic as it passed. In later years, after I was married, a house was built on the lot where Woody's garden had been. That neighbor of Dad's pestered him until the tree with my hollow was torn down. She was afraid a wind storm would damage her house.

Very often on summer days, my travels would take me to the Furnace Street side of the Iron Works and to the large windows that were always open. Peering through those windows, one could gaze across the huge open space inside. On the other side of the room, opposite the windows, to the far side, were 3 or 4 huge coal-fired furnaces with open doors. Through those openings, you could see the glowing red and orange flames leaping, ready to melt the material for molding. The material to be melted was called pig iron. I am not sure where the name came from, but it was transported from Buffalo by train. Bars of "pig iron" were heavy, weighing 80 to 100 lbs. apiece, and it was difficult manual labor. The bars were used to fill those huge furnaces for melting. First, the large bars of pig iron were unloaded from the railroad cars. The railroad siding where the iron came into town was about ½ mile from the foundry. The men would unload the iron onto vehicles to transport across town from the railroad to the foundry. Dad again, as one of his many second jobs, helped unload that pig iron for 50 CENTS A DAY. Once arrived at the foundry, it again needed to be handled by the men. The fires in those furnaces had to reach a temperature of over 2,200 degrees F. The men positioned themselves in front of those openings, ready to process the molten iron. Large bucket-like containers would hold the raw iron over the fire until it was ready to pour. The bucket was then tipped, pouring its' contents, sparks flying into long-handled ladles. The handles of the ladles must have been eight to ten feet long between the worker and the ladle to be filled. Ready on the opposite side of the room from the furnaces, on the floor under the windows, would be several wooden boxes. The boxes were filled with a sandy material prepared with pre-determined holes punched into the sand, ready for the molten iron from the huge furnaces. The molten iron was then quickly transported from the open doors of the furnaces across the room. The hot molten iron was then poured into the boxes on the floor. Then, the sides of the boxes were always tapped. Tapping made sure that any air bubbles were eliminated. Then, the iron was allowed to harden, forming door handles, hinges, castors, draw pulls, and hundreds of other items. Once hardened, the boxes were taken apart, and the contents separated. The formed product was then transported to the sorting room for final hand inspection before sending   to customers.

My mother's father worked in the sorting room for many years. My mother had a brother who worked as a pattern maker for the foundry. I have some trivets that he designed and made for my mother. Many other families in town had generations of workers employed by the foundry.

The foundry used much of the lower spots of land they owned around town to deposit its waste from the process. Many places today, when excavated, find what was called slag. Slag is the leftover pieces of hardened iron. Also, part of the deposits included the left-over cores. They could be rubbed together and sifted into sand.

Summer would find us kids standing outside the open windows watching the men stripped to their waist, muscles glistening with sweat as they carried long-handled ladles filled with the molten red iron. No matter how hot the temperature was, they were always clothed in long pants and long, heavy aprons. I would suppose that was to protect them from burns caused by boiling molten iron that would spill over the buckets as they carried them across the floor to the waiting sand molds. I can only imagine the OSHA protections that would be in place today. Dad did work there, but I do not remember that. Dad did not work there long and soon left in search of something better.

Dad always had great strength in his hands and upper body. Even as the Parkinsons took the use of his legs, that upper body strength developed from his manual labors served him well. There was also a time, however, when, as he worked at the foundry, the molten iron splattered a piece into his eye. I have no idea what was done to ease the pain, but it must have been horrific. Just one more event in life, he needed to **"suck it up."** Perhaps that was the event that prompted him to quit working at the foundry in Westmoreland. Dad told me that the day he quit, Mom's brother told her that he quit before he could get home to tell her. I do know that years later, he had what was described as "a flap" of scar tissue removed from his eye. He described it to me as being difficult. He had to remain awake and keep his eye open for the surgeon to separate piece by piece the flap from the eyeball until the surgeon could separate it totally.

The foundry owned several houses in town. Most of the men who worked at that foundry rented and lived in what were called *"shophouses."* Some of those houses were on East Main St, but most were located on Furnace Street. They have since been sold to private owners, and many still stand today. My fathers' pride hated the idea of renting from *"the foundry."* Dad purchased a building lot with a land contract from Woody on Main Street, Westmoreland, NY. I think perhaps he paid Woody for the land in labor.

Mother loved the home they rented on the main street. I don't remember ever being in it. It stood just up the road from the corner of Furnace and Main, and Mom told me once that she had not wanted to move down the road to the lot that Dad had purchased. In later years, though, she loved the home they made together and was happy with the idea that it was almost across the street from her mother and father.

Dad had his eye on an old building standing about ½ mile away from the purchased lot on Main Street.

Stu Swingruber on roof of building to be
moved

Relatives and friends ready to help move building
to Main St. Location

Building and crew ready to move building to Main St

Using Woody's beautiful team of draft horses, some round logs, and help from a group of friends that building was moved across the landscape to its new resting place on Main Street. The trip to its new location required crossing the railroad tracks, then through the fields, passing the front of Woody's barn. And across the garden, up the slight hill to its final resting place.

Swingruber kids w/ Woody's horses

Tom and Neil at the site of the "dream home" relocated onto Main St. 1945

Dad's dream home had been used for coal storage near the railroad tracks. Stu was determined to convert that old coal bin into his dream home. Once relocated, Stu proceeded to tear apart and build up the home where he raised a family and lived for the next 55 years. That building has changed hands since dad's death but is still occupied.

Main Street Home at the time of Stu's death

Esther, Stu and roses at home on Main St.

It was quite a celebration when mom got running water and then hot water. Her mother never had running water in her home. I learned at a very early age how to prime the hand pump at her large white kitchen sink. Once primed, water flowed as one raised the handle up and down.

Gramma's kitchen was a large square room. It looked like a separate addition. At one time, as I understand, it had been a shop where a gentleman made violins. There was a large white sink with a hand pump at one end.

Both my grandfather and uncle Walter, a brother of Gramma's who lived with them, chewed tobacco. Gramps chewed Red Man Tobacco, and I had quite a collection of Indian Chief cards. The packages of tobacco came with cards that had pictures of Indian Chiefs. They were a lot like collecting baseball cards today. Never knew what happened to the old tin box I kept them in. The big drawback to grammas' sink was the can that was kept at the far end. That can always smelled, as both Grampa and Uncle Walter spit out the tobacco juice and the used chew into that can. Most of the men at that time chewed tobacco. When riding in the back seat of a car, if the driver had a chew of tobacco in his mouth, you would make sure the window was up. If you forgot, you were soon reminded. When the driver would spit out his juice, the wind would blow the dark brown juice from the chew into your air space.

I am very grateful that I never saw Dad "chew." I think that all of Mom's brothers did at one time or another.

"A TIME TO WEEP AND A TIME TO LAUGH."

The very first time I remember Dad's hand holding mine, I was not very big, maybe 3 or 4, and we were walking down Genesee St., Utica, NY. I knew Mom had me all dressed up, complete with those beautiful ringlets in my hair. I was happy just to be with Dad, but I wasn't sure where we were headed. That trip's destination had been my first trip to the movie theater. Having spent all of my few years in the small town, the city of Utica seemed huge, with buildings that seemed to tower over us. Most of those buildings still stand and somehow appear to have morphed with the years. The Stanley seemed huge and beautiful. That grand old building has been restored to its original glory and operates today. As I sit in the audience for an occasional performance, my mind wanders back to that first trip with Dad. Song of the South was playing, and I can still see the bright bird on the shoulder of the black man with a beautiful blue sky and butterflies all over. He was singing and whistling Mr. Bluebird On My Shoulder, Zippidy Do Dah and A Happy Place. There was also a floppy-eared bunny conning the fox and bear, yelling, ***"Don't throw me in the briar patch."*** For me, it was a happy place that, as such, through the years, has often entered my thoughts. I read today that Song of the South is considered racist. I don't know about that I just know that I get a real warm feeling when I remember that time or hear those songs. How could Dad know that almost 80 years later, Song of the South would still be my favorite movie and hold some of my warmest memories? I often find myself while working in my kitchen humming or singing Zippidy Do Dah or A Blue Bird On My Shoulder, lost in memories of Dad and a very long time ago.

Song of the South did not leave me with any racial memories, but the condition of the "migrant workers" that were in our area each summer during that era sure did. Early memories of driving by the buildings where the workers were housed by local farmers will forever be vivid. Living conditions were supplied by the local farmers. Riding by, the buildings were despicable. Nothing more than sheds, one room for a family, filthy mattresses, and straw for sleeping spilling into the doorways, people living without running water, and

I suppose an outhouse somewhere. No kitchen table or chairs visible. Only an occasional fire in the front for cooking or heat, I suppose. Dad was a fireman, and one night, he came home from a call. It seems that the building where the "migrants" were housed had burned to the ground. Dad's comment on the firemen being unable to save the building was, ***"Perhaps now the local farmer would build a better way to house them. The farmers' cows had better living conditions."***

One of the "camps" where they lived was about 4 miles from the local store in Westmoreland. If they wanted to buy something at that store, they had to walk. The journey took them past our home on Main St. We always had dogs in the yard, and they barked at anything that moved. At the time, I did not understand why each time one of the workers walked by, they would cross the street and never take their eyes off our dog sitting on his butt barking. In later years, I understood why. TV news stories of the racial unrest in the south visualized the chases with dogs through the swamps and, later, the fire hoses and dogs that were used to "keep the colored" in line. Those buildings still stood in some areas after the turn of the 21st century, no longer housing "migrants" but reminding those of us who remember of a different time.

Racial memories from childhood remembering Song of the South NO, housing for "migrant workers" yes!

Even in the early 1960s, when I worked downtown in that very city I visited as a child, I would often eat at Woolworths' lunch counter. I realized years later that the short counter vertical to the main counter was marked "colored only." Yes, still in the '60s.

I know that Dad held my hand long before I can remember because Dad and Mom would laugh as they retold the story of my birth. Seems it was a hectic time for the third child to be on the way. They stopped partway to get Dorothy, Mom's sister-in-law, as they thought perhaps they would need her help if I made my entrance before they could make it to the Utica hospital. Dad often told of how it hurt when they crossed some railroad tracks as Mom grabbed him by the collar during a contraction. Ordinarily, this would not be too big a deal, but it seems that Dad had a full-blown case of the mumps, and at the age of 30, he was understandably uncomfortable. Years later, I realized that not only did Dad hold my hand as I took my early breaths, but he held my hand in his final breaths as he died.

Mom had just told all the ladies in the room that Dad would not be in to see her or the baby because he had the mumps when his grinning face peaked around the curtain. With a grin, he announced that he needed to see his baby girl. They laughed when they told me the story. Dad thought he was quite smart, but Mom did not think it funny on a maternity ward in 1942. The first indication of me inheriting stubbornness would be there in the hospital. Mom said that in addition to my hurry to get here, the first time the nurses brought me to her, my ankles were taped. When she asked why, she was told that it was because I would scrub them together as I cried impatiently to be fed.

The piece of land Dad purchased was located across a field from Leonard "Woody" and Rose Wood's home. Woody's house had a large attic with panels that hid spaces under the rafters with wooden sliding doors. Mr. Wood told me once that those spaces were where slaves were hidden on their trek north. I have never been able to find historical proof of that story, but as a youngster, I used to like to imagine it happening. I have recently found stories about the Masonic temple (a former church) being a stopover for the underground railway. Both Woody's house and the Masonic temple have burned to the ground, so I guess I will never know.

Rose and Leonard Woods home from our yard

Dad used to plow that huge field between our house and Woody's house next door.

Neil, Judy, and Tom w/ Woodys' horses

Dad did not plow with a tractor in 1945 but with the big pair of plow horses that belonged to Woody. I can close my eyes and feel Dad's big hands grabbing me at the waist and swinging me up onto the back of one of those big plow horses.

Neil, Judy, Tom and Woody's horses

Since I always wore a dress, I can still feel the prickle of their hairy back on my legs. Whenever one of todays' huge tractors with eight or ten plow bottoms behind comes into view my thoughts float back to dad. A young man with strong muscular shoulders and arms glistening with sweat from the sun. The reins to the horses would be across his neck and right shoulder, then under his left arm so that both hands could be on the handles of the single-blade plow attached to the horses. He spoke to those horses in a special language the animals understood. Gid-up, whoa, gee, and haw as they went one row at a time. Switching at the end of the row and heading back, turning over the deep brown soil, preparing it for Woody to plant his garden.

Woody maintained a huge garden on that acre lot. Once the plants were up, my brothers and I would be paid to get a box of garden snakes from a spot full of snakes near the woods. The boys had made a wooden box, maybe about 18 inches square. The top was a framed screen on hinges that latched down. It had handles on all four corners so that two of us could carry it once we had captured the snakes. At one time, there had been a creamery near the railroad tracks with a pit where the whey would have been discarded years before. The whey was the watery excess left from making curds. That pit was always full of snakes; we would catch them and place them in our wooden box safely secured with a latched screen top. Those snakes would then be let loose in Woodys' garden to control the bugs. This was an early form of organic gardening, I suppose. I am sure my brothers got paid, but I never knew how much or what it was spent on. Maybe a comic book or two, as in the 1940s, boys traded comic books as well as marbles. My brothers played marbles with the other boys in town. Beautifully colored glass Marbles were a prized possession. Always with my brothers, I would watch. A circle would be drawn in the dirt, each boy placing some marbles in the middle. Then, one by one, each boy would try to knock the others' marbles out of the circle. Shooting was accomplished down on one knee. Using his pointy finger and thumb, he would flick his marble along the ground from outside the circle, trying to knock out one of the others' marbles. An Aggie was especially prized, larger than the others, and often more colorful. Marbles were always kept in a soft fabric bag with a drawstring top.

Dad never made me feel like there was something I couldn't do or accomplish because I was a girl. His grit and determination were passed on as a part of my heritage. I was always with my brothers or my dad doing things. I guess Dad let me grow up ahead of the times. Although I always had dolls, I never had a lot of time for them and was really angry when my oldest brother tore the head off of one. I always knew that Dad had a soft spot for his little girl. All I had to do was walk by him with a sniffle and a tear; he would demand what was wrong, and I knew I could get my brothers in trouble.

Growing up we did not have 911 or a lot of police in cars to respond. It was mostly neighbor helping neighbor. More than once, I knew that my dad would see an acquaintance who left the bar up the street in need of a ride home. Dad would make sure that he got home safely. We had a neighbor with a large family who had a weakness to spend too much time at that bar up the road. Occasionally, one of the boys, usually late in the evening, would arrive at our kitchen door. They would be there to get dad because their dad was not treating their mother the way he should. They knew Dad would help calm the situation down. As he grew older, it was hard to remember Dad as the strong man of his younger years. In his 80's, the Parkinsons had taken most of his dignity and leg strength.

Fred and I were at a high school dance in October of 1959 when Dad came into the cafeteria where we were having a soda. It seemed that he was bleeding when he urinated and was headed to the hospital. He wanted to talk with me before he was admitted. Dad left, and Fred took one look at me and knew I needed to go to the hospital. As we arrived at St. Luke's, we found out that Dad had a growth on his kidney. Surgery would be the next day for the removal of the growth. As Fred and I left Dad's room, my brother followed us out. It seemed that Dad wanted to talk to Fred without me. I had no idea what it was all about, but after the visit, when Fred returned, he told me that Dad had just wanted a cigarette. Remember, it was the 1950s, and Fred always wore white socks and loafers; his shirt collar was always turned up, and Dad knew Fred would have a pack of cigarettes rolled up in the sleeve of his t-shirt. Dad's tumor was diagnosed as malignant. The doctor removed the entire kidney. The doctor told Mom that if it were to spread, it would go to the lungs first. For many years, Mom held her breath when Dad would have his annual X-ray. The doctor told Mom and Dad that he would most likely be out of work for six months. He returned to work, however, in 6 weeks. ***His cancer never returned***.

Years later, Dad had injured his knee and put off having the required surgery. When we spoke with the doctor after the surgery, he told us that he did not know how Dad had even stood on that knee, let alone walked on it. He said that he had had to pick Dad's cartilage out in pieces due to Dad's usage. While recuperating from the surgery, Dad would put on one of his hip boots tied around the top so he could take a shower.

Dad loved to bowl, and for several years, he bowled in a league on Friday nights. Sometime in 1972 or 3, Dad had some terrific pain in his right arm and shoulder while bowling. He finished bowling and headed to the emergency room, where he was told it was just bursitis. Dad had previously experienced a bout of Bursitis and told me he knew the pain wasn't bursitis. In the morning, he saw a heart doctor and was told he had suffered a heart attack, and the damage could be heard in the doctor's stethoscope. The doctor put Dad to bed at home and instructed him to stop smoking.

During his time in bed, his 3-year-old granddaughter Kathy was a sketch. First, she would help herself to get some grapes from the refrigerator. She would then march to the bedroom where Dad was resting. Once there, she would sit on the back corner of the bed with her back to Dad. She would then peer over her shoulder, grinning, and tell him, ***"I got your grapes, you know."*** It was an amusement and diversion we all needed.   When Dad healed and was headed back to work, Mom was really miffed at the doctor because he would not give Dad a disability release from working. It was probably a good thing for Dad to get up and get going again.

When we would go hunting, Dad was always careful with his gun, breaking it when crossing fences. The wire fences usually had four rows of barbed wire strung tightly between the fence posts. I fondly remember his strong hands holding together two levels of barbed wire up and two down. Just enough space to allow me to scoot through between them and into the fields.   Once through the barbed wire, we often found ourselves within the confines of a pasture with a herd of cows.

My apprehension about those large animals was always eased by Dad's calm with them. He would speak to them in a soft, deep tone that seemed to tell them we were not a threat.

The fence of the neighbor's pasture was right up to our yard. For at least one summer, there was a big bull with deep rust-colored spots and long horns. I think he enjoyed terrorizing me by snorting, lowering his head, and pawing at the ground under the fence. I would not go to that side of the house while he was there, and the bull would not leave, that is until Dad came home. Dad would walk up to that bull and holler. He would ask that foolish bull**, "What do you think you're doing?"** clap his hands, and tell him to get back home. When Dad hollered, that bull would turn and trot back toward the barn. I would swear with his tail between his legs. Dad would fix it, and I could once again spend some time in my swing hanging from the big old elm in my backyard. Dad explained to me that a farmer puts a ring in a bulls' nose because that is the most sensitive place. By doing so, you could lead a bull by that ring without any hesitation. Today's farming is so different than it was then. Today, very few farmers keep a bull. Most hire artificial insemination.

On a clear spring morning, Dad and I would take a walk. The feed mill was just up the road, a short distance from our home. It was a large barn building with a grinding mill on the second floor. The farmers would bring their harvest to be ground. The mill took up two floors with the milled grain dropping into waiting sacks on the lower level. I always loved the smell of the freshly ground feed. The brightly colored bags of feed were stacked, ready to be sold. Many of the girls sported new dresses made from the feed bags once emptied and washed. Dad and I would walk up to the mill, and I would listen while Dad talked with almost everyone there. He seemed to know everyone in town. The majority of the men would be farmer friends of Dad. It was on those trips that Dad would purchase the rope necessary for my swing in the big old elm in our side yard. There was a large branch that was just the right size and height for a swing. Once back home, Dad would somehow throw the rope over that limb to fashion my swing. I would spend hours in that swing.

One day, when Dad had been out hunting alone, we could see him walking bent over across the field behind the house from the woods. That field was wide open pasture stretching a long way from our house to the woods beyond.   Something did not look right and finally we could see that he had his belt around the neck of a female deer guiding her in toward the house. He surmised that dogs had run her until she lost her sight but in that blindness the doe had trusted dad to lead her. Woody's large barn was still standing, and Dad settled her in the hay loft. He called the game warden but was told to let her loose to be at the mercy of the dogs. I do not know what happened to that deer, but I know my dad could not allow her to become dog meat. I think that she was just worn out and most likely died a peaceful death in that hayloft.

It seemed that if we had a question about an animal, Dad would have the answer. Our neighbor just got up and moved, leaving her pets. One of her birds with beautiful markings ended up frozen in the ice on our pond that winter. We called Dad because we did not recognize what this bird was. Before the internet, Dad was our resource. When we described this bird to my Dad, he knew without looking that it was a Muscovy but warned that they could become aggressive and bite, so be careful. My daughter and I laid belly down on the ice to rescue the animal. With Dad's advice, we had secured the duck's bill before proceeding to free him. We were able to find a home for the duck. Dad had been correct; it was a beautiful Muscovy.

Stu w/ Chief and Mingo

In later years, Dad had two English settlers, Chief and Mingo. One evening, when my husband was out of town on business, Dad appeared at my door. He had his dog, Chief, with him. It seemed that Chief had lost a battle with a fishhook, and it was embedded in his bottom lip. Dad was there for me to hold the dog so he could force the fishhook through the lip, clip the barb, and remove the hook. Chief trusted Dad so much that I was able to hold him without incident while Dad pushed the hook through the lip, clipped the barb, and completed the removal.

Dad began my days of rescuing animals many years before. At one time, I had found a small cottontail rabbit that had been separated from its mothers' nest somehow. Dad cautioned me that wild rabbits did not live in captivity. He did, however, build a small cage for me to keep it in while I fed it from a doll bottle. It did grow and lived to be let loose that summer.

All of the lights were on, Dad's car was in the driveway, and our neighbor, Dad, and our dog were on the porch with quite a bit of blood. We had been shopping for groceries because the family was leaving first thing in the morning, boat in tow, to spend a week on an island in the St. Lawrence River. While we were gone, our dog (Goober) had been hit by a car and quite badly injured. The driver had not stopped, but our neighbor, hearing the noise, picked her out of the road and moved Goober onto our porch. He had then called Dad. Dad spent some time working with Goober and seemed to think she would live. Dad offered to take her home with him and tend to her while we were on vacation. We agreed and left for camp the next morning. No cell phones at that time so we would leave the island by boat, go into town where we would find a pay phone to call and check on our dog. Dad only said he thought she would live. He was right. However, Mom told me later that Dad had sat up all night with the dog in his lap, cleaning her wounds and encouraging her to drink. He always believed that if an animal would drink and eat, it would live.

Dad, growing up on a farm and working extra for the neighboring farmers, had to learn a great deal about treating sick and injured animals. Regular visits to a vet were not commonplace, and farmers usually treated their own. Once, when we were walking through the fields, he made a note of a plant that we call Yarrow or bone set. Big purple stems with a cluster of blossoms at the top. He said that his dad would boil that plant and feed the broth to his horses for arthritis. If you research Yarrow today, you will find many health benefits of the plant. Among those is help for arthritis in the joints. Amazing.

<u>"A TIME TO MOURN AND A TIME TO DANCE"</u>

Dad had a big white dog with black spots much like a Dalmatian. Her name was Tippy, and one day, she appeared in the driveway in obvious distress. She sat on her haunches at the end of the driveway. I will never forget her eyes and the pain they seemed to show. Dad did not know what was wrong, but he did know she was in need of help. Dad came home from the vets without Tippy. The vet had needed to put her to sleep. She had gotten into some poison, and it had destroyed her insides. Dad believed that the neighbor had carelessly put rat poison out where an animal could ingest it. It was many years before that animosity toward his neighbor faded, and feelings mended. Much later in the years that dad or mom would need an ambulance called they were some of the neighbors that would show up to see if they could help. Neighbor Marge, when Dad was pretty much housebound, would stop to see Dad and bring her cats down to visit. The many years of resentment over the death of Tippy had ebbed away with time.

The doctors at the Masonic believed that Dad had a case of Pernicious Anemia and prescribed a shot for him once a month. We would almost know when it was time for his shot because Dad would not seem quite as sharp. It is ironic that we could not get any help for Dad's Parkinsons, but because he needed a shot once a month, a visiting nurse was to come to administer that shot. It also enabled us to have an aide come once a day to do some light housekeeping and personal care. Only the Masonic doctors would acknowledge that Dad needed the shot, as Dr. O would not prescribe it for him. There was one night, Dad seemed quite distant, and Marge and Ted let Dad use Ted's oxygen for the night. I spent the night with Dad, and the next morning, the visiting nurse administered the B12 shot. The shot seemed to make a difference for Dad, and we returned the oxygen that Dad had used throughout the night.

When Dad was housebound due to his Parkinson's, he wanted a dog. I said ok, providing that we put in a fence and a dog door so that the dog doesn't need to be walked. Dad, in his stubborn way, said,

"Not by a dammed sight, I can walk the dog." It became a real point of contention between us. My phone rang one afternoon, and on the other end, Dad told me he would not take his medicine unless I let him have a dog. It broke my heart to tell him to go ahead; he was a big boy, and the decision would be his. It seems the next morning, his aide Marge called me to let me know that Dad did not take his medicine for that day, but just so I would know, the medicine for two days later was not in the container. It was a mental war between myself and Dad.

A few days later, when I made my daily stop, there was a note taped to the wall that Dad wanted me to read. It seemed that the afternoon aide that came from the visiting nurses left me a note. She indicated that I was being mean to my dad by not letting him have a dog. She said if Dad had to go into the hospital, she would take the dog and tend to him. There was no reference to a daily walk or cleaning up after the dog. I felt she was out of line but did not report it to the visiting nurse association. Nor did I tell them of the afternoon that I stopped in while she was there to find her sitting at the kitchen table doing crossword puzzles, doing nothing for Dad. She indicated that he was sleeping, and she did not want to wake him. She was getting paid to give Dad personal care and do light housework. From that day on, she made sure she did her job.

On our last trip for medical help dad let me know that he had changed his mind. It seemed that my offer to get him a cat instead of a dog was now acceptable. Our neighbor Marge had once again brought her cat over to spend some time with dad and he thought he might enjoy a cat after all. He said when he got home, he wanted a cat. It saddens me that I was never able to get a cat for dad.

As I visit Mom and Dad's grave, it seems ironic that just across the path between graves is the grave of Marge and Ted. The neighbors in life are neighbors in death.

"A TIME TO SCATTER STONES AND A TIME TO GATHER THEM"

As part of converting that coal storage building, mom and dad worked to gather cobblestones from a nearby creek. Those stones had to be just the right size and worn smooth by the movement of the waters. The stones were taken home and used to build a fireplace in their living room. When they built the fireplace dad used mortar between the stones. He told me once that his father had learned as a young boy in Switzerland how to lay up a stone wall that would last for years without any mortar.

Years after Dad's death, we were able to travel to Switzerland. As we traveled across the countryside and up into the mountains, dads' words echoed while witnessing the long stone walls built without any mortar.

Rock wall in Switzerland

As kids we spent a lot of time around the ponds and lakes swimming, and fishing. A favorite pastime between splashes was to find a flat stone. One that would fit in the palm of our hand. This always resulted in a competition. Dad had taught us that if we threw the stone the right way, it would skip across the water. The competition was to see who could get the most skips before the stone would finally plunge beneath the water's surface. Would it just sink, or would it skip off the surface of the water two, three, or maybe four times?

"A TIME TO EMBRACE AND A TIME TO REFRAIN FROM EMBRACING"

My ears still ring with my Brother Neil's screams as he was being thrown over the bank and into the water. Dad's hands had his wrists, and our older brother Tom had his ankles. They began swinging Neil back and forth in anticipation of throwing him into the water. He was afraid of the water and did not know how to swim. They had decided it was time he learned how one way or the other. I do not know how he got out of the water or if the experience taught him to swim because, in the terror of a 5 or 6-year-old, I had scrambled up the bank from the creek and hid on the floor of the back seat of Dad's car. I heard them calling, looking for me, but did not answer out of fear that I would be next. They finally found me, and even though they assured me that I would not be next, I did not trust for a long time. I did, however, become determined to learn to swim.

Neil had been VERY ill as a toddler and spent eighteen months in bed in an attempt to cure Rheumatic Fever. The doctor that treated Neil was Dr. Rudolph Vandevere, a fairly young doctor who practiced in Rome, New York. He had a medicine that was relatively new in the area. Mom listened to a lot of criticism because she put her trust in that new doctor and his prescribed drug called Salicylate. Salicylate had been invented in the late 1800's and was a forerunner to today's Penicillin. It was used to treat the inflammation of the joints caused by Rheumatic Fever. Others gave Mom a hard time keeping Neil in bed and said let him go; let him play.

Mom's fear of Rheumatic Fever had been exemplified by the fact that one of Dad's brothers had died as a young man of 30 from the same disease. Charles had become disabled and had to move in with Gramma and Grampa Swingruber. When he died, he left a widow and two daughters who lived with Dad and his parents when Dad was young. Charles' death had compounded the situation that forced Dad to quit high school. Mom also knew that Dad's sister Helen had died from Rheumatic Fever when she was only 14, two years before Dad was born. Even once Neil was allowed out of bed, Dad still carried him to school and up the steps to get him into his

Stucco school where Neil attended

Classroom. The school at that time was a large grey stucco building. Once you entered the front doors, you had to go up the steps to get to the first-floor classroom. At that level, there was a large open area with classrooms on each side. There were also stairs up to the second floor and stairs that went down to a gym area. I understand that Dad's anger was stirred when he heard that when the other kids went out to play, Neil was locked alone in his classroom. Mom said that dad made short work of making sure that Neil was never left locked alone in an empty classroom AGAIN.

Neil grew up to be quite a talented athlete. Baseball pitcher, basketball, and football consumed his high school activities. In later years, he played in what he called old man's softball and adult pick-up hockey. He loved to play golf and often played with his son and sometimes with his dad and Fred.

When Neil started high school, he wanted to play football, and mom said no. She was afraid the Rheumatic Fever had damaged his heart. The high school coach, a family friend, and a one-time neighbor thought he should. Dad finally convinced mom to let him take Neil to a new group of doctors. They were starting a practice in the area. It has since evolved into a huge clinic. Dr. Dickson and Dr. Slocum would evaluate Neil. The Drs said they could find nothing wrong with Neil's heart but could not say definitely that he would not have a problem playing football. Dad and Coach Page convinced Mom that Neil would be okay with just going into the game to kick. Needless to say, Neil got in and was allowed to do much more than kick. He became a really good high school player. Mom would not go to a game, though, as she was terrified he would have a heart attack on the field. We lived close enough to the football field that she could hear the crowd, and every time she heard a roar, she was sure Neil had been hurt. Years later, as a grown woman, I was helping mom in the kitchen. It was then that I realized the old brown bottle on the top shelf of her refrigerator was the last empty bottle of Neil's salicylate. Mom was a worrier until the day she died and always had a soft spot in her heart for **"My Neillie".**

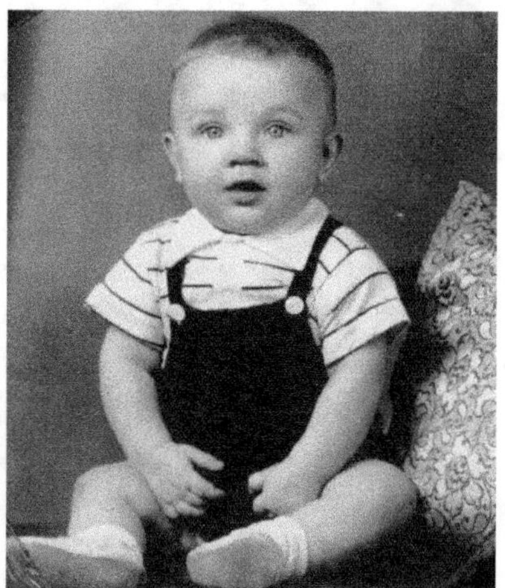

In the winter, Dad, my brothers, and a lot of the boys in town would shovel local swamps or ponds to be able to play hockey. There were no youth sports leagues, just the town guys getting together. Dad, Neil and some of the neighbor kids flooded the town green one year so that hockey could be played. Dad loved hockey and was always a willing participant with those pick-up hockey games.

Nobody wore helmets; shins were protected by taping magazines and newspapers across them. The blades of hockey sticks were reinforced with lots of black tape, and we played hockey. My brothers always promised me that if I helped shovel, I would get to play. Needless to say, their idea of play was to stick me in the goal where nobody ever got a shot at me because one of my brothers would always skate in front of me.

Stu ready to play hockey

The big event in the area was a local hockey team, The Clinton Comets, in Clinton, New York, and Dad loved to go to the games. Years later, Dad's youngest granddaughter worked for the Utica Devils, and the team was bringing in Gordie Howe. Wow, what an event! Kathy was able to arrange for Dad to meet with Mr. Howe after the game. While standing in the lobby watching Dad and Mr. Howe pose for a picture with Kathy, all seemed to be going well. Suddenly, my father had the nerve to jostle and elbow Mr. Howe. Before I could speak, Mr. Howe responded. Instead of being offended, Mr. Howe grinned and jostled back. Dad and Mr. Howe had a great time. Gordie Howe, the great legend, a fantastic hockey player, but an even greater human being who took the time to laugh and jostle back and forth with an old man that loved hockey.

Kathy, Stu and Gordie Howe

It seems ironic to me that the first time I can remember my brothers' voice was one of terror, learning to swim the hard way. The last time was as he lay dying in a hospital an hour and a half from my doorstep. DeDe Neil's wife had called me to let me know that Neil had a stroke and was in Albany Medical Center. It was in the middle of the COVID-19 pandemic, and she was not allowed in to see him. She said the doctors and nurses were good at speaking with her and keeping her updated. At that time, I was spending ½ hour once a day on my treadmill listening to tapes of Alan Jackson. Neil had been in the Intensive care unit about a week. I was very deep in prayer while on my treadmill, asking God to be with Neil and help him get better. Alan Jackson was in my ear singing I'll fly away. Suddenly, the music stopped, and Neil was there, a shadowy vision on a light background. He was saying, ***"I am tired Jud"***. I found myself short of breath as I said, 'You need to fight Neil. We need you; DeDe needs you, but he just said I am just so tired, over and over. I remember then telling him he needed to fight like a Swingruber, not a Dowsland. Moms' family seemed to have a low pain threshold and dads was as high as it could be. I was only thinking of the tolerance for pain, not meant to demean

Mom's family. It was then that I realized that Neil's shadowy vision had been leaning against another. It was Mom. She was there holding *"her Neillie"* and helping him move beyond. Just as the words were out of my mouth with one more, ***"I'm so tired, Jud,"*** the visions whisked away. First, the vision of Neil turned and moved beyond, and then the vision of Mom turned and faded quickly into the distant light.

As soon as they disappeared, the music started again, and I heard Alan Jackson sing "I'll fly away". I know that people will think that I was hallucinating, but I know what happened. As I stopped my treadmill and got off, I was crying, sick to my stomach, and shaking. I was weak, knowing that I had to do something! Neil knew of my faith, and he had let me know he needed to let go. DeDe had to be with Neil! He needed her to be at his side. They had married as kids straight out of high school and had stayed together for almost 65 years. I e-mailed the hospital and heard back right away. The hospital had a special way that spouses could be in the Intensive Care if death was imminent. Not knowing what to do, I paced the kitchen floor, thinking and talking with Fred. Finally, after a few minutes of frustration, I put in a call to DeDe. She answered right away and said, ***"I can't talk now. The hospital just called, and we are arranging for me to go to Neil"***. I received a text the next morning that Neil had passed. DeDe was able to be with Neil as he left us here on earth. After Mom's death, I was often aware of her presence with me. Not anymore; since she and Neil left, I have not had any awareness of her. Perhaps someday she will forgive me, and her spirit will return. The sound of Neil's voice that began in terror ended with peace. He knew of my faith and that he could let me know he was ok.

Thank you, Neil; God loves you.

Judy and Neil, October 2011

<u>"A TIME TO SEARCH AND A TIME TO GIVE UP"</u>

Dad had a typical old hound with short legs, floppy ears, and brown, black, and white markings. It was great fun to hunt rabbits with him ahead of us, letting us know he was in the scent of a rabbit. Our old hound Mike would sound out loudly when on the trail of rabbits. There was a hunting trip with Mike one fall at a location a few miles from the house. Mike had been barking loudly when all of a sudden, he just stopped. The air went still. Unusual for Mike; he would not answer Dad's calls. We waited quite a while, and then Dad said he was ok and would go home. I cried, stormed around, called Mike, and insisted that we keep looking. We could not go home without Mike. Finally, Dad, tired of my tantrum, decided enough was enough; Mike would find his way, and that's where we headed! Upon our arrival in the driveway, guess who was sitting on our back porch? The look on his face was as if to say what took you guys so long. Yes, Dad had been right; Mike found his way and beat us home.

Mike

"A TIME TO KEEP AND A TIME TO THROW AWAY"

My oldest brother Toms' wife was very talented with her hands. Doris was a great seamstress, and many times, I have been thankful for her sewing lessons. Through the years of their marriage, Doris would make and send Mom pieces of BEAUTIFULLY hand-painted, 8-inch ceramic figures of the Nativity. Dad built a rough creche to hold the nativity on the fireplace in the living room.

Nativity at Stu & Esthers'

Every year during Christmas time, my daughters would spend a day with Gramma, baking cookies and putting the Nativity on the mantle. Even during the year that both Mom and Dad were in the nursing home, Kathy set up the nativity on the windowsill in Mom's room. It drew great attention from all over the nursing home, and mom took great pride in showing it off and letting everyone know that her daughter-in-law had made it and her granddaughter had set it up for her. The Christmas after Mom died, Dad finally got home from the nursing home. Kathy, our youngest daughter, spent time with

Grampa and placed the Nativity on the mantle. A few days later, as I walked into Dad's home. He was sitting in his chair across the room from the fireplace with one of the beautiful wisemen clutched tightly in his hand. I asked what was up. He told me that he had called Tom in Oregon to tell him that he wanted to get on a train and go out to visit him for a few days. Not able to get Tom, Doris had answered the phone. She informed dad that he wasn't welcome out there and Tom did not want him to come. Through measured calm, he told me that if I didn't get the ###*** Nativity out of his house, he would destroy every piece. He only relinquished the idea of destroying it because he believed that Mom would want Kathy to have it. He made me promise that Doris would never get it. Sadly, I removed the entire Nativity and delivered it to Kathy, who still cherishes it, with great memories of spending time with her gram.

Nativity at Kathy's

"A TIME TO TEAR AND A TIME TO MEND"

Part one

After Dad left the foundry in Westmoreland, he went to work for a factory in Whitesboro, NY, sometime in the early 1950s. Dad worked the night shift, and sometime in the night, the phone rang. Mom received the news that Dad had had an accident at work. The plant made blades for jet engines, and part of Dad's job had been to guide the piece of metal into position for the massive hammer to drop onto it, forming the piece of metal into the necessary shape. A cord was attached to Dad's wrist. It was supposed to make sure his hand was retracted before the hammer dropped. Dad said he had told the bosses that it was not working right, but as of that time, it had not been repaired. As a result, the hammer dropped, catching the end of Dad's pointing finger on his right hand. Dad was able once again to rely on his high pain tolerance, and in quick thinking, he removed the tip of his finger before heading to the hospital. The co-worker who drove him to the hospital had not been able to bring along the fingertip. Dad, however, had the forethought to remove the tip of his finger and take it to the hospital in hopes that it could be reattached. Dad was in the hospital a few days and came home with a cast on his forearm and over the back of his hand. There was a wire attached between the finger and the cast to hold it steady as it healed. The tip of that finger was forever after bent at that first knuckle and the nail always had a split. I never heard him complain, nor did it ever seem to stop him from doing whatever he pleased.

September 1, 1961, arrived. It had been a beautiful day, and as evening approached, Dad and I were in the car headed to the church where Fred and I were to be married. I couldn't believe all the cars parked along the road on our way. Mom had gone on ahead, and as I entered the narthex of the church filled to standing room only, mom greeted me. I will never forget the first words she spoke to me that evening; ***"Well Judy, I guess this is goodbye"***. At 19 years of age, I was not prepared to think that it would be goodbye. I turned to Dad and said, ***"Did you hear what she said? Is it goodbye"?*** He patiently explained that no it did not need to mean goodbye. It only meant that the circle of family needed to open our connection and add to the chain. Soon after that the music began and dad and I started up the aisle to the alter where Fred was waiting. As we rounded the corner and walked between the pews, something happened that I had not anticipated. The hem of my gown was wider than the space between the pews, and I had stepped on the front of my dress. Without a moment's hesitation, Dad's hand reached out and took hold of the front of my skirt, lifting it just enough for us to continue to the front of the church and to my wedding.

So, often as my family has grown and moved on Dad's words have comforted me, especially on the day that our oldest daughter arrived home from her honeymoon and was packing the U-Haul to move 500 miles away with her new husband. It had been a beautiful wedding, and I had been reassured as Paul held Jennifer's hands as they recited their vows. But now, as I stood on the porch watching them pack, I did not want them to go. Then Jenn slowly came up the driveway to me for one last goodbye hug. We stood embraced together, trembling. Remembering Dad's words, I whispered, ***"Don't cry; if you don't, I won't."*** It was Dads' strength that allowed me to open the circle and hold back the tears until the U-Haul was out of sight.

Jen and Paul on their way to VA and new life

It had been a snowy winter day at the beginning of January when I suddenly stepped through Mom and Dad's kitchen door and collapsed sobbing in my father's lap. It was only four months since Fred and I had been married and things were going great. Mom and Dad were alarmed as all I could say was, ***"he's dead,"*** over and over. It had been snowing all day, and the roads were not very good. Earlier, Fred and I had been at Mom and Dad's house waiting for them to get home from my brother's. Neil lived a couple of hours away; the roads were slippery and I was concerned for their safe trip home. While we waited for my parents, unexpectedly, Arvie, the best man at our wedding, stepped through the door. He had some bad news. All he knew was that Fred's dad had suffered a heart attack, and they were on their way with him to the hospital. Arvie navigated our way through traffic for a hurried trip to the hospital. As we walked through the hospital entrance, his sister wailed ***"He's dead, I'll never see my father again."*** We had not gotten there in time to say goodbye. We had spent the prior evening with Fred's mom and dad and had no suspicion that he was ill. We left the hospital and went to Fred's parents' home with his mother and his sisters. Trying to stay strong for Fred and his family, I took our car to get gas, leaving Fred with his family. After getting gas I found I needed to make a stop at home, to be with the people that had been my sanctuary for so long. Mom and Dad finally got me calmed down and realized that Fred was fine; my new father-in-law had suffered a heart attack and, at 57, was dead. Dad held me long enough to let me regain my composure, enabling me to return to Fred and his family calmly in their time of need. Once more, Dad and Mom had been there to help me **"suck it up."**

"A TIME TO TEAR AND A TIME TO MEND."

Part two

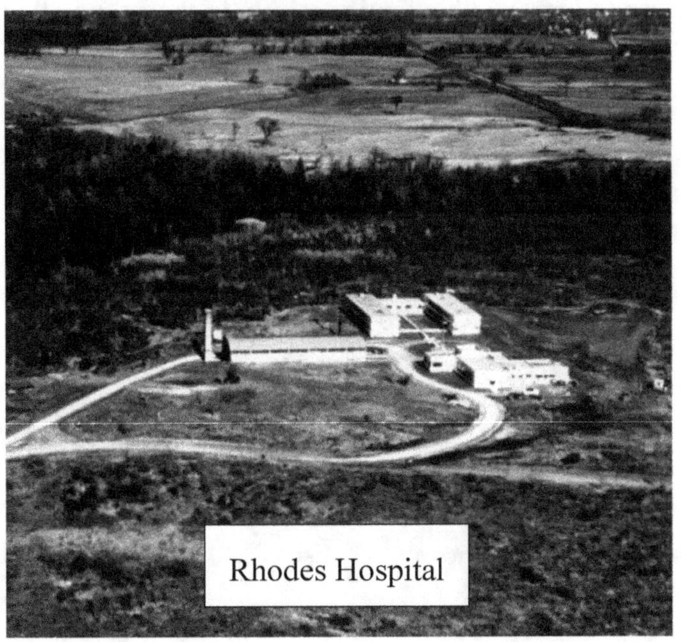

Rhodes Hospital

Sometime in 1942 Rhodes Hospital facility was built and opened in Oneida County about 10 miles from my parents' home. It became one of the great orthopedic hospitals of the war. It was an active-duty post that included enlisted men and officer quarters, a chapel, motor pool, access to telephones and post office. There was also a theater, chapel laundry sewing and carpenter shops.

The Red Cross had one of the 100 buildings on the site, and it was the only two-story building. Nurses and doctors served on the active-duty post. The aim was to return soldiers to active duty. Counseling and religious services were provided for servicemen of Catholic, Protestant, and Jewish Faith. Construction costs were estimated at $44,000,000. The facility had a railroad siding built especially for handling the arrivals of the 25,277 wounded soldiers from North Africa, Sicily, Italy, France, and Germany. The government disbursed $25,000,000 for necessary supplies, products, and food, and $175,000 monthly salaries.

The Rhodes Hospital was named after Army Surgeon Col. Thomas Leidy Rhoads an Army Surgeon and was created for patients who needed convalescent care. **[1]

As the war wound down the hospital dispositioned its last patient on June 30 of 1946 and was no longer needed. After all that expense it was declared "government surplus" In 1959, 20 acres of the site were made available to the Syracuse Diocese of the Catholic Church. The Notre Dame High School is currently located on those 20 acres.

When the "hospital" was no longer needed, the buildings were converted into housing. That became a turning point in my dad's life. I will never know how Dad found out that there was an opening for a job helping the electrician re-wire the buildings, but Dad realized a real affinity for understanding electricity. That job opened a whole new world for him. For many years, Dad took on extra jobs, wiring houses and camps and converting old buildings. One building that I especially remember was what we called the Spagen house. I spent a lot of time with Dad, helping him re-wire that old building, making it usable for the local school district. The three-story building fascinated me. It had originally been a stop on the stagecoach line through the village. In the basement, the old brick ovens were still visible. Bricks are standing floor to ceiling, almost wall to wall, in that section of the cellar. There were openings in the bricks that must have been used for baking and cooking for the tavern. A wide hallway on the second floor with rooms off to each side. They would have been rooms for overnight travelers as they passed through town. This building was converted and successfully used as a schoolhouse for a few years. I attended 4th grade in a room on the second floor with lots of windows that looked out onto the main street. This building was positioned

---

**[1] The Utica Observer-Dispatch 10/29/2009 and The New Hartford Historical Society

between the gas station on the corner and the Westmoreland UM Church.

Dad had learned electricity at Rhodes and later became employed at the very factory where his hand had been hurt. There he enjoyed the title of head maintenance man in charge of their electricity. One can hardly forget the day he came home from work and told us that he had the job that day of searching on top of the (generators) for a bomb that was threatened at the plant. Dad was fascinated with the idea that there was a thing called the internet that would someday allow him to connect with his eldest son on the West Coast.

<u>"A TIME TO BE SILENT AND A TIME TO SPEAK"</u>

Who would have thought that anyone would ever take a letter from an eleven-year-old girl seriously? That afternoon, as I walked through the kitchen door, Dad was waiting for me. Sitting at the kitchen table, his coffee cup in hand, his first words were, ***"Judy, have you been writing letters?"*** I had forgotten the handwritten letter of an eleven-year-old to the town board. A letter telling them that it was not right for our town to be without a Christmas tree when all the towns and cities around us did. It seemed that Dad had gotten a phone call that afternoon, and we were to attend the board meeting that night. Dad did not let me know if I was in trouble or not. Off to the meeting, we went with my hand in his. I was certainly wishing that letter had not been sent and that I had kept silent. When we arrived at the town meeting, supervisor Murphy seemed quite jovial, and I began to relax.

One of the second jobs Dad held in previous years was to plow snow for the town so everyone seemed to know him. He often spoke about handling the wing of the plow to push the snow back off the banks to the edge of the road. He decided to quit that job the spring I was born. The previous winter he had waded through waist deep snow to get to the town barn where the plows were kept.

Supervisor Murphy introduced us to the board and proceeded to discuss "the letter." Everyone seemed to think that it was a great idea to have a town tree. There was just one catch. That catch was that my dad would take care of picking out the trees and getting it decorated. With that stipulation, the town approved $25, a year for decorations. Remember, it was 1953, and prices were not quite what they would be today. We would need to go to a local stand of evergreen trees. Pick out a tree, cut it down, and drag it to the edge of the trees. Once we selected a tree, the highway crew would transport it and set it up for us to decorate. We were able to have quite a beautiful tree as Dad did business with an electrical store and was able to get his discount applied. Mr. Levine, the owner of the business, laughed at my letter and donated two beautiful blue angels to be lit on the top of the tree. Dad, my brother Neil, and later my fiancé Fred took care of that tree for several years. In 1961, in the fall, when my wedding was scheduled, Dad said that it would be the last year he would take care of the tree.

The town has since planted a tree on the green. It is not as big as those we hauled out of the woods, but it will grow. They leave the lights placed on the tree so they can just turn them on during the Christmas season. I often pass through the village during the holidays and see the tree with its red, green, and blue lights a glow. It brings back fond memories of lugging a huge tree, ladders, snow, decorations, and times with Dad.

'A TIME TO LOVE AND A TIME TO HATE"

Dr. Katz with gramma

I am not sure what it was that awakened me. The streetlight outside always gave partial light in the house at night, but tonight, many house lights were on. After my mother's father died, her mother (Lottie) lived with us. She slept with me in my bed, but I had not been aware of her getting up. Mom had made me sleep on the side of the bed next to the wall so Gram could get up to go to the bathroom if necessary. The lights were on, and there seemed to be quite a bit of commotion. I rounded the corner of the kitchen door to see my father on the bathroom floor next to the bathtub with my grandmother across his lap. His sleeveless undershirt had blood spatters. He was pressing hard on the back of her head. There was also another man in the room, down on his knees. It seemed that in the late fifties, at that time in the world, doctors made house calls. The other man on the floor was Dr. Katz who had arrived from his office in Clinton, a town about 10 miles away. I watched as he instructed Dad to hold the wound on Gramma's head closed while he took a stitch and then to let the pressure loose, allowing the blood to spurt. I watched a few stitches completed and remember feeling that Dad had everything under control and went back to bed. I found out later that Gramma had fallen in the bathroom, hit her head on the bathtub, and had a nasty cut in need of several stitches. I assume Dad helped Gram until Dr. Katz arrived. I do know that without those big, powerful hands of dads to assist the Dr., I am not sure what would have happened. I just remember two men, a tiny elderly woman, the middle of the night, and a lot of blood.

Gram needed to spend a few days in the hospital after her fall. While she was there, two of Mom's sisters-in-law went to see her. During their "visit with Gram," they convinced her that she would never return to her home and that they should go into her home and give away her belongings. Mom was upset, and Dad was angry.

I had spent many hours in that big warm kitchen of grammas'. There was a large white sink with a water pump in the corner by the back door, her table and chairs in the middle of the room, no electric iron but an actual iron that sat on its side on her huge cast iron stove with a water well on its side. There was a big, soft couch nestled in the corner where I could sit and look out the window. There were glass shelves hanging against that window with two little lambs, one black and one white that held her small green ivies. I remember looking through those glass shelves across the road to Mom and Dad's house years before as they moved into our new home. Out of that window, I was able to watch Grampa's large Hydrangea tree leave out, bud, and blossom into a profusion of snow-white blossoms. This day was different. It did not feel like a warm and happy place as I sat on the couch in Gramma's kitchen with Aunt Dorothy. Dorothy was the widow of grammas oldest son, who had passed away, and she was also upset. Suddenly, Dad burst through the kitchen door and yelled at those "cleaning out gramma things." I had never heard Dad quite so angry at anyone over anything before in my life. At the top of his lungs, he yelled, ***"What in the hell do you think you are doing? This is hers to do."*** Unfortunately, they did not listen and simply continued to divie up the lifetime of Gramma's belongings. Unfortunately, I lived to see Dad proven right. Gramma came home from the hospital to live with us. Grampa had passed away on memorial weekend and sometime that summer Gramma and I were alone in our house. Gramma took my arm and said, ***"Come on, Judy, we are going to take a walk"***.

My grandmother was not even 5 feet tall and must not have weighed 100 pounds. She always wore her grey hair pulled straight back in a bun at the back of her head. Mom said it was dark and curly in earlier years and thought perhaps that was where I inherited my curls.

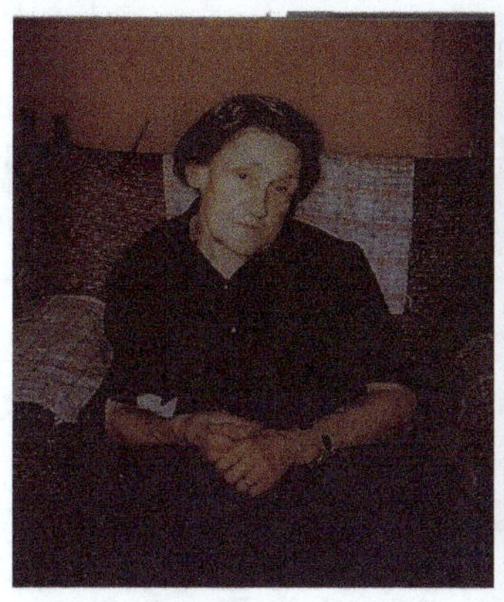

I accompanied Gramma along the road about 500 feet. We then crossed the road to what had been home to her and Grampa. I do not know how long Gramma and Grampa had lived in that house on Main Street in Westmoreland, New York. As long as I could remember, it had been grammas'. A place I loved and where I spent a great deal of time. I would not call them rich by any means. Actually, by today's standards, they would be considered poverty. No running water, a chemical toilet in the back shed, and no central heat but her whole life was in that building. Everything she owned and had collected since her marriage to Grampa in 1900. Her years of marriage with the man she had loved and where they raised a family. It is with indescribable sadness that I remember the look in her eyes as she stepped through the door. Empty kitchen, no table, and chairs, no pots and pans or dishes, or silverware, no sofa, dining room empty except for an old sideboard, the bedroom that she had shared with her husband of over 50 years stripped. Not even a sweater or shirt of Grampas' to wrap herself in. ***<u>Nothing left to cherish</u>***. Not even the curtains on the windows or her old stove with that iron resting comfortably on its side. **<u>All</u>** of their belongings had gone to destinations unknown to her. She turned to me and said**, *"Judy, let's go home"***. At 15, I had all I could do to keep up with her as she moved as fast as her 82-year-old legs could go. Later that day, Mom just said to me, ***"I heard you took a walk today, Judy"***.

My gramma never went back into that house again. She would often be seen looking out Mom's kitchen window toward it. One can only imagine what her thoughts and memories were as she sat in Mom's kitchen gazing out that window toward the past that had been so cruelly stripped from her so quickly. When my aunts visited Gramma in the hospital and convinced her to give up her possessions, her only stipulation was that I should have my choice of dishes and her oldest grandson should have the mantle clock. I chose her ruby glassware that, at that time, had very little value compared to her china. Mom tried to get me to take the china. I think that the china and the clock had been from her family at the time of her wedding. I have no idea where the china went but the ruby red pitcher and glasses adorn the top of the buffet in my dining room that belonged to my fathers' mother. Alan took the clock, and I am glad to know where that went. Dad had tried but was outnumbered by the wives of Gramma's sons. After they thought they had stripped Gramma's house clean and left there were a couple of items they missed. A pink vase and that pair of lambs. Small lambs, one white and one black, that Gramma kept on those glass shelves in her kitchen window. Those lambs safely rest in my china cabinet now with cherished memories of long ago.

There is an old adage that says time heals all wounds. I am not sure about all of them, but the one between my dad and his mother-in-law certainly did. Mom was only Eighteen years old when she and Dad were married. Dad, five years older, had lived and worked the family farm since necessity made him leave school at 15. He had been planting and taking care of the livestock and the fields. He felt that he had earned his keep, so he and his mom moved in with Gramma and Grampa Swingruber. Mom was the youngest of seven children and the only girl. Mom's mother was not happy with her only daughter's place of residence. According to Dad, she made it quite difficult for Dad and Mom to stay there. Mom felt that she did not have any privacy at the Swingrubers. I think that Dad's mother, after having 8 children of her own and helping to raise some of her grandchildren, was not very understanding of an eighteen-year-old new mother and the wife of her youngest, very special child. Eventually, Mom's mother got her way, and Dad and Mom moved into the small apartment in the Dowsland home. Needless to say, Dad was not happy with the situation, which was aggravated by some of Mom's brothers. Dad was very prideful and always wanted to be sure he paid his own way. The date they were able to move to their own residence is unknown. They were married in 1934, and for a while, they lived in a house Mom called the house "up street." From there, I understand that in 1943 or 4, they moved into the converted coal barn where they lived the rest of their lives. That home was almost across the street from mom's mother and dad. There were several times that Dad would help out. Gramma did not have a phone, and when she needed something from our house, she would turn on the porch light at the kitchen door. That kitchen door faced the road and had a cement walk from the road to the door. There was an apple tree beside that path that had green apples with a splash of red on its side when ripe. Grampa called it a Maiden Blush tree, and I can still see Gramma peeling apples. She always wore a dress and an apron. She would sit on the back steps with a wooden bowl in her lap between her legs. I have that wooden bowl, and as I dust it, fond memories of Gramma fill my mind. She always peeled   with a paring knife and peeled the skin so thin you could almost see through it. Always in one continuous peel. To the day he died Neil talked about gramma's apple pies.

Gramma and Grampa Dowslands' home in
Westmoreland

Many times that light would have mom and/or dad scurry across the road to offer aid. One time in the late afternoon, I looked out Mom's kitchen window and knew something wasn't right at Gramma's. The light was on, and something was on the ground outside on the kitchen doorstep. Dad and Neil moved quickly across the road. When they got there, it seemed that Grampa had suffered a heart attack and fallen on the stoop. The doctor was called, and Mom was told that Grampa was in better shape than Gramma and she might not live the night. She did, of course, as her sole purpose in life to take care of the man she had married in 1900, so many years before.

Grampa had what was then called dropsy. Today it is labeled edema and often accompanies congestive heart failure. The doctor would come every so often. I understand that he would "drain" the fluid that would collect around Grampas' ankles. I never witnessed the procedure but was told it was very painful. I am sure that modern medicine would have a better method of treatment. Until that day, there had not been a phone at Gramma's house. Imagine today without a phone.

From that day on, the only time I knew Grampa to leave his bed was for Dad and Mom to take Grampa to watch grandson Neil pitch a baseball game.

Fred and Lottie Dowsland front porch

Fred and Lottie Dowsland Fred
bedridden

Neil Swingruber High School Baseball

Grampa loved baseball; he coached a Westmoreland team, and his sons and son-in-law all played. While Grampa was bedridden, Dad had been the one Gramma asked when Grampa needed shaving or other things I am sure a man needed to have done for him while he was bedridden. I never heard Dad complain about doing such. Long gone were the early days and the resentments. Six sons, five still

81

living, and the one whom Gramma felt she could ask was her son-in-law. Grampa died on Memorial weekend in 1957. And it was after that that Gramma came to live with us. During the time Gramma was with us, my mother realized her mother's need to care for someone and stepped aside, letting Gramma take care of my dad. Gramma took over the task of making sure that Dad's coffee and a snack were ready when he came home from work.

Esther Swingruber w/ Mother
Charlotte Dowsland 1958

With today's phones, it is hard to imagine a party line where you could listen to the conversations of a half dozen other people. When Grampa had his heart attack and was bedridden, Mom picked up the phone to hear two of her sisters-in-law talking. They were saying that it was too bad that the ***"damned old drunk had fallen and ruined their Christmas Holiday."*** Everyone knew that Grampa liked his drink, but this time, it had not been the case. Hurt, Mom said nothing; she just hung up the phone.

There is a very vivid remembrance of Dad and Mom having a really heated argument. It was over me and an experience that I had with my mother's father. Mom had gotten me all dressed up with my hair done, especially in those long black ringlets. She had a real knack with my hair, turning those natural curls into beautiful ringlets down my back. Grampa had taken me to the local bar to show me off to his friends. Dad was not happy with his little girl being put through that experience and made me promise never to go near that place again.

75+ years later, the uneasy memories of Grampa lifting me up onto the bar in front of his buddies to show me off remain. The local bar up the road was nicknamed the Bucket of Blood and sat in a small hollow off the side of the road. It was dirty and dark, and my experience with my grandfather was the only time I was ever there. To this day, I am not sure if it was the experience, Dad's reaction, or the combination, but I have never entered a restaurant with a bar without recalling that feeling. I am VERY uncomfortable to this day when in that atmosphere. Grampa didn't mean harm; he was just showing me off to his buddies. For years after, when I walked up the street and had to pass the "bucket," I crossed the road. The hollow in the road has now been filled, and there is a new thriving restaurant and bar in place of "the bucket." As I pass the location today, I often think of my promise to Dad.

It was a beautiful spring morning, Easter weekend in 1959 when I was alone with Gramma when she died. For three or four months off and on, I had experienced a recurring, disturbing dream. Each time, it was the exact same one. It would picture Gramma's death just as it eventually happened. I had avoided being alone with my gramma, that I loved. In my teenage mind, I believed if I avoided her, she would not die. On that morning, since I had my driver's license, Mom had me take her to my brother's so she could tend to my nephew. I was then to go back home and wait for gramma to get ready so I could also take her to my brother's home. Gram and I sat at the kitchen table for a while. She was holding her head as she often did. She had Glaucoma, and it usually made her eyes hurt. Gramma then got up and went into the bathroom. When I heard the noise, I knew exactly what had happened. It had appeared to me so many times in my dreams. Gramma had a heart attack and fell crumpled under the sink. I called Dottie, our neighbor, and held Gram till she and David got there. It then became my job to go and tell my mother that Gramma had fallen, and I didn't think that she had lived. Dottie asked me later how I knew what to do. All I could say was I dreamed it.

After Grammas' funeral, everyone was at our house, as was custom in those days. That day, the aunts that had said the nasty things about Grampa, the very ones that had given away all her things, were there laughing and talking. I could see my mother's hurt at the phone call. I could see the look in Gramma's eyes as she entered her empty home. I remembered my father yelling at those very women. It seemed to be more than I could bear. Welling up with anger and fighting back tears, I turned and barged through the door into my mom and dad's bedroom. Stopping short, I realized that Dad was sitting on the end of their bed, his head in his hands, and for the first time in my life, I realized Dad was crying. I had never seen my dad cry. It seemed that no matter what the situation, he would ***"suck it up"***, be strong, and not show emotion.

As I said I do not know if time heals all wounds, but I believe that it had between this man and his mother-in-law.

"A TIME FOR WAR AND A TIME FOR PEACE"

Dad was born in the years just before the First World War and was too young to serve. By the time the Second World War was raging, Jessie, dad's older sister, was married with a daughter, Helen, and a son, Robert. Helen, born in 1922, and Bob, born February 3rd, 1924, grew up across the lot between Dad's home and Jessie's. Dad was closer to Bob than any of his older brothers, and I was told that Gramma held a special place in her heart for her "two" boys. One son born late in life, and one grandson always together.

Jessie told me once that Bob walked through her door on December 7th, 1941, the day the Japanese bombed Pearl Harbor, and told her he was going to quit school and go to war. He enlisted in the Marines on December 17th, 1941, and at 17 and 18, saw things in the Pacific theater that no teenage boy should ever see. Things of war that lingered within him for the rest of his life. Dad told me once that Bob was transferred to DC while suffering with a case of Malaria he caught while overseas in the Pacific Theater. The effects of the Malaria always seemed to linger in his health. That summer before his discharge, the Atomic Bomb was dropped on Japan. Looking back, I believe that at the time of his discharge on December 18th, 1945, he suffered from what would now be called PTSD. In the late 40's and 50's, it was not yet labeled as such, and there wasn't a great deal of support for returning veterans. Our Vets mostly had to struggle and ***"suck it up."*** Many of our war heroes, including Bob, came home as heavy smokers.

United States Marine Corps

Robert E Frey Discharge Paper

Bob and Dad always shared an unbreakable bond. In later years would share replacing a roof or furnace or just Bob and Betty playing cards and enjoying an evening with coffee and pie. It was a sad day when we heard that Bob's previous bout with lung cancer had returned. There was an inoperable growth around his heart, and the cancer had metastasized and spread to his brain.

Robert E Frey

Jessie, Helen & Bob Frey

By the time of the news, Dad's Parkinson's disease had greatly diminished the use of his legs. He got around for short distances with a walker, but for a longer distance traveled in a wheelchair with help. I took Dad on his last visit with Bob at the hospital. Bob's room was in the older part of the hospital and the room had been darkened and seemed dingy. It was as an intruder, I listened from the corner and witnessed firsthand the love between two old friends. The talk about "Uncle Stu" teaches a young Bob to handle a gun, shoot his first pheasant, and bag his first deer, along with many, many memories. Happy memories, reliving the many times they shared together in their youth, continuing into the waning years of adulthood. Knowing that they would most likely never be together again here on earth, tears rolled gently down my cheeks. Then, as the time came to say goodbye, "Uncle Stu" struggled to get from the wheelchair to his feet. I watched in amazement as, without a walker or any support struggling, he pulled himself up, standing as straight as his Parkinsons and arthritic-ridden spine and hips allowed. He then snapped to attention, and with his stiff right hand, the veteran was saluted by his one-time mentor. My tears continued as the stoic old man in his wheelchair was guided through the hospital halls to the car. Once more, Dad had had to **"suck it up."**

I do not remember if Dad was able to make Bob's funeral, but I do remember the dark sky, the Marines in their striking dress uniforms, the firing of rifles, and the somber sound of taps echoing throughout the quiet, grey cemetery. Then, with the precision of the marines, the precisely folded flag was presented to Betty. Years later, Betty, Bob's wife, told me that after Bob died, she found a baby picture of me in his wallet. I was born during the time Bob was overseas. He had carried my picture during his service in the Pacific and to his death. No one had ever realized how special "Uncle Stu's little girl" had been to a young soldier through the terror of World War II.

Judith Margaret Swingruber 1942

At Christmas there is a wreath with a red bow gently laid in remembrance and gratitude at Bob's grave. Hopefully those two long-time friends have found each other in Heaven and can once more share old time memories.

"A TIME TO BE BORN AND A TIME TO DIE:"

Part two

It is not clear to me a specific time when the roles were reversed but it is not fun when you realize that you have nearly become your parents' parent.

It was at his granddaughters' high school softball game in 1988 when Dad first asked me what I knew about a disease called Parkinson's. At the time, I had little knowledge, but over the next dozen years, a lot was learned. At first, Dad managed it pretty well, but as time progressed, so did the disease. Little by little, slurred speech, facial masking, drooling, paranoia, and limited mobility developing over time robbed a proud man of his self-sufficiency.

The local doctors that dad had did not seem to be helping him a great deal. He hated his medicine as it that made him sick to his stomach, and the local doctor said that he must take it as there was no choice. I am not sure how we found Dr. Stuart Factor at the Albany Medical Center. He was a specialist in Parkinson's disease. For Dad's first appointment, our daughter Kathy accompanied me because it was very difficult for one person to get Dad out of his wheelchair. We took an instant like to Dr. Factor because he treated Dad like an intelligent human being. The first thing he did for Dad was change his medicine. Telling Dad that there was no reason for the medicine to make him sick to his stomach. It never did from that day forward. Under Dr. Factor's care, Dad progressed to the point that Kathy was no longer necessary to help us with doctor's appointments. Dad was finally able to get out of the wheelchair and get around without help.

One thing that bothered Dad terribly was the fact that he was unable to control his drooling. It was awful; one day, when I was tying Dad's shoes, he leaned over to tell me something, and his drool dropped onto my head and oozed down my forehead. We never talked about that incident, but I know it bothered Dad more than me. When we discussed this issue with Dr. Factor, he said he would like to try something different. He explained that the use of Botox could possibly freeze the muscles that made Dad drool and would we like to try it? Both Dad and I were in agreement. The Botox worked. 1 injection every 3 months or so, and Dad no longer drooled. I find it amusing when the ads for using Botox products to soothe a person's wrinkles appear on television. It always makes me thankful for the medicinal purpose of Botox that helped Dad so much. When Dad was in the hospital the last time, I received an irritating phone call. It seemed that a Dr. was on the other end of the call, wanting me to change from Dr. Factor to him as Dad's specialist. It was with great satisfaction that I reminded the man that he had been Dad's Dr before we went to Dr. Factor, and he hadn't been able to help Dad before, and we would stay with Dr. Factor for medicines and advice.

The Parkinsons had caused his legs to become very stiff and difficult to walk. In order to get in the car, he needed help to swing his legs inside. With the same tenacity he had had all his life, he refused to accept that he should no longer drive. One afternoon, as I pulled into the driveway and walked to the door, he was standing in the doorway. Both of my brothers were there. They were standing behind him, and I think they were expecting me to be the heavy. I believe that they had told Dad that I was the stumbling block to him being able to drive. Speaking across the porch as I approached, he announced to me that we were going to go for a ride. I said OK, where were we going but one of the boys or myself was going to drive. He said, ***"NOT BY A DAMNED SIGHT HE WAS GOING TO PROVE TO ME THAT HE COULD DRIVE"***. When I said no, he said he could, and what did I care if he smashed up the car and killed himself? I had to draw on that tenacity he had passed on to me and tell him I did not care if he killed himself, but I did care if he hit a mother walking her baby on the side of the road. He proceeded to inform me that if that was what I was going to do, ***"I had better be damned well ready to take him anywhere he wanted to go at any time he wanted."***

It worked out pretty well for a while, as I was able to take him to see mom at the nursing home every day. However, one day, I was unable to get there and told Dad we could not make it that day. I received a phone call that afternoon from the nursing home. Did I know that Dad had driven himself to Utica, to the nursing home, alone? I quietly said no and asked them to let me know when he left. I then asked his neighbor to let me know if she saw Dad drive in the yard. The calls came in. He had made it home safely. I have no idea what happened. We never spoke about his trip, but very soon after that, he indicated that he wanted Fred to sell his car as he wasn't going to drive anymore. As usual, it had to be Dad's decision.

Dad's doctor, O., and I did not get along. He was dismissive of my presence in Dad's life. Dad's illness was having a strange effect. He was beginning to tell me about seeing things that were not there. He thought he saw bears across the road in the neighbor's yard and mice under the chair in the doctor's waiting room. We had an appointment scheduled, and as usual, Neil came to my rescue. While I waited, Neil attempted to give Dad a shower. That had become quite a chore. Neil would put on his bathing trunks and get Dad into the shower. It was during the shower that day that Dad had somehow lost his balance and slipped. Neil had tried to break Dad's fall, and he was sitting on the bench in the shower, holding Dad, keeping him from falling completely onto the floor. Dad was stiff, unable to bend at the waist, and was standing upright, leaning across Neil at an angle that did not allow Neil to get him up. That is when they called me for help. In order to help Neil get Dad's stiff body into an upright position, I laid stomach down on the bathroom floor, braced my feet across the room against the toilet, and, with my arms stretched out, braced my father's feet, keeping him from slipping forward. That enabled Neil to get Dad standing upright. Just one more indignity for a grown man having the need for not only his son but his daughter to help him in the shower.

It was for that visit that Neil and I took Dad to his appointment with Dr. O. He walked into the room, shook hands with my brother, turned his back to my outstretched hand, and began to speak with Dad. Dr. O., as he shall be referred to, finished examining Dad and did not seem to think that there was any reason for Dad to be there except to discuss Dr. O's sons playing hockey. When I asked about Dad's lungs, he sarcastically asked me what I thought was the matter with them. I indicated that I felt his breathing was a little raspy. He turned and, for the first time, put a stethoscope on Dad's chest. He listened for a short time and said, ***"MY GOD STU, YOU HAVE***

PNEUMONIA." Not a word to me but told my brother that he would need to admit dad to the hospital.

Dad was in and out of the hospital every so often, and each time, they would need to start over with his medicine. They would not let me bring in his medicine from home or even continue the dosage he had taken that day. As a result, he would often miss his medicine and become confused. The change in medicine and the paranoia of the Parkinsons often caused a great deal of angst.

It was during that trip for Pneumonia to the hospital that Dad tried to get up on his own during the night and fell. No one, including Dr. O, took the fall seriously, and no one ordered an X-ray. After a few days, which included some physical therapy, Dr. O decided it was time to release him to rehab. My many experiences with The Masonic Home in Utica proved it to be a fantastic facility. Dr. O did not like me placing Dad there as it is a closed facility, and their staff doctors take care of the patients. The day after his admission for that visit, we had what they call a team meeting. At that meeting, Dad's physical therapist told the team that Dad had a problem. He had known Dad from previous times and always found him to be a fighter. The PT told us that Stu just couldn't work through the pain this time. We agreed to an x-ray, and I headed home. My trip from the Masonic usually took me a little over ½ hour. I stopped for a couple of simple errands, and as I walked through my door, the phone was ringing. It was the Dr. at the Masonic. In the length of time it took me to get home, an x-ray had been taken and read, and the results indicated that Dad had fractured his hip when he fell in the hospital. The hospital and Dr. O. sent Dad to PT, where they proceeded to have him walk, opening the fracture beyond repair. The Dr. from the Masonic was telling me that Dad was already on his way to the hospital for a hip replacement. Dad would not let me take any action against the hospital or the doctor. Having the power of attorney, however, I went to the hospital and requested the paperwork from Dad's visit. They wanted me to let them mail it when they could get to it. I refused, indicating that I would wait. It took a while, but sure enough, when I received his papers, there was a notation that indicated Dad had fallen and reported pain, but no follow-up had been ordered.

Mom was scheduled for open heart surgery on the first of April 1996, and Dad was to have surgery for an Acute Aortic Aneurysm (AAA) on April 15th. Mom was in the cardiac care unit waiting to be transferred to a hospital an hour and a half away. No one except Mom had talked to a doctor, and none of us had any of the details. Mom was terrified, so I went to the hospital very early and waited for her heart doctor to make rounds. I was hoping to get some information about her condition. Much to my consternation, her heart doctor was not on call, and Dad's doctor, O, came into her room. He was aware that I had power of attorney and HIPPA authorization for both of my parents. When I asked him a question, he said, ***"I'm not her doctor, and I won't talk with you."*** Since Dad, his patient, was also scheduled for surgery, I proceeded to try to ask about Dad and his upcoming surgery. He answered, ***"I told you I will not talk with you,"*** turned on his heels, and walked away. We received no information from anyone until Mom was admitted into her room at the hospital in Albany. Dad and the rest of the family were at the hospital in Albany. We had been there a while, hoping to speak with the surgeon, and the others decided to go to the cafeteria and get something to eat. While alone with mom in her room, the surgeon appeared. His words will never be forgotten. He said, ***"Esther, I am sure that I can get you through the surgery, but I am not sure that you will be able to get yourself better."*** Sometimes, seemingly harsh words ring true. Mom came through the surgery but was unable to make herself cough and accumulated fluid in her lungs. The very Dr. who spoke those words to her that evening came into the hospital on Easter Sunday to suction her out and perform a tracheotomy on her throat.

Dad, in the meantime, had bet me a dinner that he would be home from his aneurysm surgery within a week.

Dr. O. was called in to position a Swan catheter in Dad prior to his Aneurysm surgery scheduled for the next day. My brother Tom was at the hospital with Dad and filled me in on some of the details a few days later. It seems that after Dr. O was finished, he left the hospital. A nurse realized a problem with the catheter placement and called on another dr. to reset it. No one was notified, and there was no notation in Dad's file. It was obvious, however, that Dr. O. had made an incorrect placement. Dad made out fine, and Dr. Caeser told us in our post-op conference that it was too bad that Dad had Parkinson's because his organs inside reflected a man 15 years his junior. Dad once more won his bet and was released from the hospital on the 7th day. He was right and was home from his surgery before Mom was transferred from Albany to Utica.

It was a beautiful August morning and Fred and I were enjoying an early morning cup of coffee at our pond. I had been at the hospital with dad for quite a while the day before and was enjoying a quiet morning before heading back to the hospital.

Dad had needed to go to the urgent care at the clinic a couple of days before, and the doctor on call had summoned Dr. O down to see Dad. His breathing was labored, and he was having difficulty swallowing. Dr. O had Dad admitted to the hospital. As usual, the social worker at the hospital cornered me in the hall and said I needed to have Dad transferred to a nursing home. She was pretty insistent that it should not be the Masonic. Simply ignoring her insistence, I gave her the name of the lady at the Masonic who had helped us out so many times before.

It had been almost 2 years since our youngest daughter's wedding and she was nursing a nasty broken ankle. She could not drive so I went to her house to pick her up. She wanted to purchase some special groceries for their anniversary. While waiting for her to finish getting ready I noticed a book on her side table. It was one of the Chicken Soup for the soul books.

There was a story about a man that planted trees and subsequently refused to water them and daily went out and beat the trees with a stick. When asked why, he simply said I am not going to be here forever and the trees will need to live on without my watering them or staking the trees against the weather and the wind. They will need to stand alone.

In his own way, I think that Dad's father had treated him like that and, in turn, Dad his sons. There were times in life when you had to just *"suck it up."* For me, his little girl, that toughness was passed on but in a different way. I believe that the same kind of grit that brought 17-year-old Grampa Fred here so many years ago was passed to Stu. That legacy of strength and determination is now visible in all following generations and threads within us all. Reflections on my life with my daughters make me realize that that kind of grit applied to their lives was probably misunderstood just as generations before.

When Kathy and I got to the hospital, Dad was in trouble. His lungs were filling up with fluid; he was strangling and having great trouble breathing. As I arrived at his bedside, he grabbed my arm and *"said you've got to help me."* When respiratory therapy finally showed up, they said the only thing that they could do was to suction his lungs. With the condition Dad was in, it seemed incredible to me that they even had to consider whether to do it. Once several cc's of fluid were removed, Dad was again comfortable. Fred came to the hospital, saw Dad for a few minutes, and took Kathy home. I stayed with Dad for a while, and he talked and talked. We spoke about mom, his dogs, his mother, the early years of his marriage, and his family growing up. He spoke about the times of the Second World War and the horrors that were reported in the newspapers before the attack on Pearl Harbor. Dad told me of a Nazi organization in Yorkville, a few miles from home. He seemed quite comfortable, and I traveled home somewhere around nine.

Once Fred and I finished coffee beside our pond, I headed back to the house to shower and get ready to head to the hospital to check on Dad. As I entered our back door, my phone was ringing. It was early, and I sensed that it would not be good. I was right. It was the hospital letting me know that Dr. O wanted to see me at the hospital as soon as possible. Getting showered and dressed took me about 35 minutes to get to the hospital, where Dr. O was impatiently waiting for me. He informed me that Dad was in bad shape and the next step would be a ventilator. Even though he knew Dad had a DNR, he made me make the call to no ventilator.

The last time I picked Dad up from the rehabilitation unit at the Masonic, he told me that he did not want to go home. When I asked him where he wanted to go, he said, ***"I want to go and be with your mother."*** I told him that I wasn't able to help him with that, and we proceeded to take him to the home he had always loved.

I got so I hated the phone ringing because it usually meant that I would be out the door. Ever since mom's open-heart surgery either mom or dad would need the emergency room every other week or so. Mom's condition after her surgery kept her in the hospital in Albany for a couple of weeks and then many weeks in the local hospital. The damage had been done to her swallowing muscles by feeding her when she had a trach. She was unable to eat solid food. She had been allowed to stay in bed without any attempt to get her up and walking as she had refused to try. Her food was administered through a food tube inserted into her nose. She was transported to another hospital for a fluoroscope. As a result, that hospital recommended trying "thermal therapy" in order to strengthen her swallowing muscles. No one at the facility she was in had any knowledge of the therapy, and a lady from the second facility had to come and show us how. The nurses at the first facility did not want to be bothered even to learn, so my brother and I managed to administer the therapy.

Thermal therapy is a relatively simple procedure. A long handled instrument that looks like a dentist mirror is kept in a container of ice. The instrument is then used to tap on the inside of the throat on both sides causing the swallowing muscles to react and strengthen. We tried to accomplish this at least 3 times each day.

During the time that mom was hospitalized, I had been summoned to the hospital to meet with my brothers, dad, and the head of the physical therapy at the hospital. As the last to arrive, it was explained to me by the head of the hospital PT unit that since mom was unable to walk, there was only one way for her to return home. The only way that would be possible was for me to learn to use a Hoyer Lift. I indicated that a Hoyer lift was not an option. I lived 5 miles away and could not be available each and every time Mom needed to be moved. I told the PT that if he taught me what was needed, I would get her up and walk. He laughed in my face and indicated that it would be impossible. He was wrong! It was a struggle, and it necessitated every bit of that tenacity that I had inherited. My mother was about 125 pounds overweight and not terribly easy to motivate. The PT did, however, explain what would be needed. At first, it was just getting her to sit herself up, then take a step or two until she was able to manage a walker. From that facility, she was released to the Masonic Care Facility, where they proved to be fantastic. They understood all about thermal therapy and continued to rehabilitate her eating and walking. After weeks in the local hospital and in the Masonic Care Facility, both had been accomplished, and she was to be released to go home without a Hoyer Lift and on a regular diet. Finally, she and Dad would be back together in their home for so many years.

Since mom still had a trach, in order for her to go home, someone had to learn to suction out the trach. The procedure required learning how to put on sterile gloves and insert a suction tube into the trach to remove any mucus formed there. Dad, Neil, and I learned to do the procedure, but Mom was afraid to have Dad do it. His hands were stiff from rheumatism and Parkinson's. They made it difficult for him to put on the required sterile gloves necessary to perform the procedure. Mom was afraid to have him put the suction tube down her trach. Neil was about 1 and ½ hours away, and as a result, my phone often rang. I would travel to their home about 5 miles away to remove the clot of mucus that was blocking her airways. This would most often happen during the night.

One afternoon, as I stopped in, Mom had refused to get up out of her recliner at all that day. Once again, calling on my stubbornness, I was trying to make her get up. She sat there shaking her head, and I became really insistent. I looked up just in time to see that big fist of my father's drawback stopping inches from my nose. He hollered at me to stop being mean to my mother. WOW, it took every bit of strength for me to say, ***"Go ahead, but when I pick myself up from the floor, I am out that door, and you will never see me again."*** He relaxed, Mom got up, and it never came close to happening again. It is the only time that I can remember Dad close to striking me.

I became very fond of Wednesdays. That was the day that my brother Neil would come from his home about an hour and a half away and take care of whatever mom and dad (and later just dad) needed that day. Wednesdays were the day I was able to make any personal appointments knowing that Neil would be there. I always knew when Neil headed home as my phone would ring about an hour later.

Dad was in and out of the Masonic Care community and hated every minute of his stay. Not because they were not good to him but just because he wanted to be home. In order to get Dad released from the Masonic, we needed to prove to his review committee that he would be safe if he were discharged. It took more time than Dad was willing to put up with, and he became very agitated with me because I could not get him out of there and home. During one visit a day or two before our daughter's wedding, he approached me to go home with me. He intended to sleep on my couch the night before the wedding. Our oldest daughter, her husband, and 3 kids were at my house, and it was just not a possibility. Neil was going to come up and take Dad to the wedding. Dad informed me that if he couldn't stay on my couch, he wasn't going to go to the wedding. In anger and frustration, he threw a bag of Hershey kisses across the room. Not realizing that his bag of Hershey kisses was open when he threw it, the candy scattered across the room and over my head while he screamed at me to leave. I took a deep breath and did not start to cry until I was out the door and down the hall. The tears continued all the way home to where our girls were starting to put together the table decorations for the next day's wedding without me. They were frustrated with me because I was so long at the nursing home.

Later that fall, we were able to put together a plan that satisfied Dad's committee, and Neil and I took Dad home. I don't think that I had seen him that happy and content in a very long time as he settled into his recliner in his own living room,

Part of the plan to get Dad home was for him to agree to wear a notification device. This was in case he fell or got in trouble, and he could push the button and get help. I was to be the first person called, a neighbor second, and the firemen as a last resort. Neil would come and get Dad for the day on Thanksgiving and Christmas. The first Thanksgiving went well, and we were looking forward to Dad's first Christmas home, even though it would be without Mom. Dad spent Christmas Eve with Fred and me at our house, and I took him home to sleep and wait for Neil in the morning. We had settled in bed when the phone rang and the person on the other end told me that Dad had pushed his alert button, ask her to call me, be sure to tell me that he was ok but he needed me to come down.

Not knowing what to expect, I headed for Dad's. Dad had built the cupboards for Mom's kitchen years before. Along the outside West wall, there was a counter without cupboards underneath. Walking through the kitchen door, I realized that the refrigerator on the East wall was tipped forward, resting against that counter at an angle, pinning Dad underneath. Dad had been trying to get himself some ice cream. His Parkinson's often caused him to fall over backward, unable to break the fall. In this case, while trying to get some ice cream, a Parkinson's fall had taken place. While going over backward he held onto the handle on the freezer door. The refrigerator did not hold him and tipped forward, forcing Dad under the counter. From his position under the counter, he peered at me and assured me he was ok. Not hurt, just trapped. Without thinking I reached out and set the refrigerator upright. In tipping it upright, I hadn't held the refrigerator or freezer doors closed. As a result, all the contents emptied onto the floor. Now, not only was Dad on the floor, but so were the contents of the refrigerator and the freezer. Dad first, once the frig was upright and not blocking him in, we were able to get him up and then take care of the refrigerator contents from the floor. Once settled, I got Dad his dish of ice cream, and we laughed about it all. I put on a pot of coffee, and we waited until Neil came to get Dad for the day before I returned home.

No one will ever convince me that God does not exist. There is a God. Throughout my life, I have been present at the deathbed of too many persons. My grandmother, an uncle, a best friend riddled with Cancer, my mother, and, of course, my dad. After Mom's death and through the last months of Dad's life, we shared his struggle, his pain, his loss of dignity and his need to ***"suck it up."*** I had often prayed that he could just lay down and go to sleep, and God would take him home. Being human however, when I would walk through his door, I would dread that perhaps my prayers had been answered. Each time though, God had said not yet, Judy and Dad and I would just **"suck it up"** another time.

During one of my remembered conversations with dad he told me of the time when he was recuperating from his kidney operation. At that time, the removal of a Kidney required a large incision across his back and a lot of internal disruption. He was in a great deal of pain. He believed his mother, long before, in the arms of God, came to him and told him it was not his time yet and he needed to continue with life. The doctors had told Mom to expect Dad to be out of work for 6 months. He returned to his job in 6 weeks.

Years later, our church had a new minister, which, in retrospect, was providential. He was only with us for a few months, but I believe that he was supposed to be with us. I took him to meet with Dad, introduced them to one another, and left. After completing my errands, I returned, and the minister was gone. He had not stayed long, and Dad did not say much about him except he seemed to be a good guy. Very shortly after the visit, the minister suddenly needed to leave our church. He had family matters in another state, and I hadn't been able to speak with him. As if meant to be, I ran into him in the local mall parking lot the day he was leaving. All he said was, **"You don't need to worry about your dad he is ok."**

Once the no ventilator decision was made, Dr. O said he would move Dad to the Cardiac Care unit where they could get Dad a mask for his oxygen, which would make him more comfortable. Dad was struggling to breathe and unable to speak. I asked him if he wanted anyone else to be with him and he shook his head no. I asked about my brother, Fred, a minister, or anyone. I wasn't sure I was going to be strong enough to get through what we both knew was ahead. I asked him if he and I were going to do this "alone," and he just shook his head.

When Mom died, the decision to take her off the ventilator and stop all artificial means to keep her alive was left to me. I had promised her that I would do that. Dad and Neil were both in the room when Mom died. That decision is one that I would not wish on anyone. After her death, when Dad was home, I was visiting with the neighbor that I called when Gram died. I indicated to her how hard a decision it had been to take Mom off life support. I told her that my head knew it was the right decision, but my heart would never be sure. Dottie, a registered nurse, had visited Mom in the hospital and understood. I did not realize that Dad had been listening. Dad looked at me and sternly informed me that the choice I made was the right one and that he *"expected"* me to do the same thing for him.

We did not have a cell phone, and while they were transferring Dad to a different floor, I tried several pay phones, and not one would connect. I could not get through either to Neil or to my husband. Each phone I tried would fill with static and squeal in my ear. I was not sure that I could do that again alone. Once Dad was settled, they tried to put an oxygen mask on Dad to replace the nostril oxygen he was getting. His Parkinsons had locked his jaws so that they could not get his mouth closed, and a mask would not work. It was then that I pulled up all my strength, and my years of church attendance reminded me of a favorite scripture. *"Mathew 18:20 __King James Bible__ For where two or three are gathered together in my name, there am I in the midst of them."*

My quiet prayer was crude but sincere. I whispered, *"goll darn you God, you promised that whenever two or more are gathered in your name you will be there. Dad and I need you here NOW."* I have no doubt that God not only heard my prayer but answered. Most people refused to believe me, but the light in the room changed. It took on a soft amber aura, and I was comforted and filled with a quiet, soothing calmness. Dad was no longer struggling to breathe. He appeared to be simply sleeping peacefully. Each breath is a little softer and slower.

Somewhere during that time, I was aware that Dr. O appeared, stood across the room for a short time, never said a word, and quietly left. Who needed him, then? As I sat at Dad's bedside holding his hand, a technician appeared to do an EKG. She attached the machine to Dad, and the monitor went crazy. The only thing I can compare it to is the old TV screens when they would go all snowy and with lines jumping all over. The screen on the monitor surprised her, and as she looked over, she realized that I was holding Dad's hand. She had been getting two pulses. She asked me to let go, and the moment I did, the monitor settled into a normal readout. Once she unhooked Dad from the machine, I reached again to take Dad's hand. To my surprise, without opening his eyes or appearing to wake up, he gently pushed my hand away. I soon realized, though, as he reached to hold my hand, that I would be Daddy's little girl to the very end. With his hand gently holding mine, I bent over and whispered in his ear, *"I love you, I love you, I love you, and I'll bet that your mother and mom are waiting for you. But just so you know, when it's my turn, you better be waiting for me."* It was at that time he squeezed the hand that he was holding. It would be the last movement or gesture he would make. Soon after, the nurse appeared and let me know that Dad was finally at peace. He had had to *"suck it up"* for the last time, and God had been there with us at the end.   My prayers had been answered. Once God came, Dad just peacefully went to sleep, never to wake again.

Two things that stand out in my memory happened the morning after Dad died. The phone rang, totally unexpected. When I answered, Dr. O was on the other end. I had briefly glanced at him when he entered the room as Dad lay dying. He went to the other side of the room, said nothing, stayed only a few moments, and quietly left. I had completely wiped his memory from my mind. He surprised me by actually sounding concerned. He asked if **I** was OK. In my surprise, I said yes but did have a question for him. Had he given any kind of drug to Dad as the situation seemed to change so completely? He said no, but he, too, noticed the change in the room and in Dad, but it was not his doing. He said he had no answer for what he saw. God had come to help Dad, and I ***"suck it up"*** without him.

Since our church was temporarily without a minister, I reached back to one who had been with us in the past to conduct Dad's funeral ceremony. Pastor MacDonald had agreed but was unexpected when she showed up at my back door. She listened intently to hear the experience of God being with Dad and me at his bedside. She did not doubt! We prayed together as we sat on our porch swing. She then asked me what Hymns and which passages of scripture I wanted to read. Then, her big question, which I was not prepared for. Who would be speaking in memory of Dad at the funeral? I told her that there would be no one. She refused to accept that answer. Our oldest brother was not going to come from the West Coast for the funeral, and I knew without asking that Neil could not do it. That left me. Digging deep, I realized that I had found the answer in the chance story read a few days before in Chicken Soup for the Soul. It made me think so much of Dad and the way he lived his life. The heritage of dads' tenacity had surfaced for me again, and one last time for Dad I was able to ***"suck it up"*** and able to try to relate it in tribute to Dad.

<u>EPILOGUE</u>

Dad often said, **"too soon old too late smart"**. How true that has proven in my life. As a child, I took my parent's love, especially my fathers' for granted, never having it cross my mind that it would not always be there. In many ways, however, that love will always be with me. For a long time after Dad's death, I had a great sense that he was with me. Just a heaviness just over my right shoulder walking with me. Then, one night, as I slept, Mom was there holding me close to her. So vivid that I could feel her warmth as she laid her head against my chest and told me, ***"it is ok now Dad and I are together."*** Since then, I no longer sense Dad at my shoulder, but he will forever reside in my heart and memory. As I grow older, it is with a realization that much of the good in my life has been the result of my dad's unyielding love and strength. I was able to find a husband who loves me, treats me with respect, and supports me in every endeavor. Without him and my brothers' support, those last two years of my parents' lives could have easily broken me. I look back now sometimes with sadness that I seemed impatient with them. I know, however, that without the generations of toughness I inherited, the struggle would have had a different ending.

I do not know of the relationship between my mothers' mother and her father. I have pictures and stories of a relatively wealthy farmer who died at a fairly young age, long before his time, the result of being gored by a bull in his pasture. I know that my grandfather's (Dad's father) relationship with his mother was to see that she arrived safely in the new world. I believe that my dad's relationship appeared to be the strongest with his mom His with his dad seemed to me to have been one of strength and reserve. Grampa Fred passed to Dad the strength and so many lessons that enabled him to ***"suck it up"*** and survive. My mom loved her dad and was always his baby girl (youngest of 7 and only girl.) The love between my father and I goes without saying. I can give my mother credit for some of that, as she always took a back seat and encouraged my relationship with Dad. The history of generations of love between parent and child is something that I will always cherish. Being eighty-plus enables me to have the history and knowledge of past generations. It also grants me a vision into the future of the generations that follow me. I cherish the evidence and importance in the bond between parent and child. My husband, father to our three daughters, has a bond so much like what I had with my father. Not to the hunting and fishing of my generation but to things of another generation with importance to their world. All three of our girls have the ability to do almost anything to which they set their minds. Our middle daughter was born with a congenital hip and spent 36 weeks, 3 days, and 15 minutes in a series of 3 body casts. Her strength and independence had her crawling all over in that body cast. She learned to carry a toy in her mouth, prop herself up to a stair, and play with that toy while upright. Such grit at less than a year old. All three, as grown women, are successful in their business worlds, raising our grandchildren, and are also able to tackle any task with determination and that inherited strength.

Our oldest daughter is now a grandmother. Her oldest son is married with a daughter of his own. That makes me a great-grandmother. Some of Addie's baby pictures look a little like me, but the most poignant connection I see is the love she has for her dad. A recent Christmas card picture of Addie shows her looking up to her dad while holding on to his finger with the love and security between a daughter and her dad. This picture of my grandson and his daughter fills me with warmth and complete serenity. I remember with fondness the security my dad's hands gave me throughout my life and even as he lay dying. I look at the picture of Addie holding her daddy's finger and am assured that the bond between Jake and Addie, his daughter, lives three generations into the future.

It is with much love and confidence that my memories of dad's hands are evident in those future generations between my grandson and my great granddaughter. The love and trust is there and will surely support her for the rest of her life.

It is my fervent wish that every daughter could have the security of Daddy's hand as I knew it!

Thank you, Dad!